Coding by Doing

For Absolute Beginners

– 2 Books in One –

Learn SQL and Python Programming

Learn Programming Fast

SQL Programming
A Beginners Guide

Learn SQL Today

Preface

This book will serve as an essential guide for you, as a SQL beginner. In addition, the concepts of SQL are laid out in a simple, concise language and instructions to help you learn the steps properly.

Specific examples and sample tables are showcased to help you practice most of the SQL queries.

Thanks again I hope you enjoy it!

Table of Content

Chapter 1: Definition and Purposes of SQL

For beginners, learning SQL is like learning how to speak a foreign language. You have to learn the alphabets first before you can successfully use it. Knowing the definition and purposes of SQL is crucial, before you, as a beginner can make any significant progress.

Looking at those symbols and queries may seem scary and confusing, but do not worry, the technical jargon is explained in the simplest manner to facilitate your comprehension.

What is SQL?

SQL stands for Structured Query Language. It is a standard programming language used in fetching or retrieving tables from databases. Other areas of use are creating, accessing and manipulating databases.

The most commonly used versions of the SQL are the SQL99 standard originally established by ANSI (American National Standards Institute). There is also an ORACLE version called PL/SQL, and a Microsoft version called T-SQL or Transact-SQL.

More people are growing aware of it because SQL is one of the easiest and most powerful methods of editing databases. It works in such a way that you can perform your tasks more efficiently, within a shorter timeframe.

The SQL's basis is the RDBMS (Relational Database Management System), which stores data in the form of tables.

What is a database?

A database is a collection of information usually contained in electronic files stored in a computer. These files are arranged and organized so data and information can be modified and manipulated in a fast and easy way.

Purposes of SQL

There are various specific purposes for using SQL. The most common purposes are:

- Accessing Databases
- Creating and Joining Tables
- Modifying and updating tables
- Deleting Data
- Reading Data

- Retrieving and Organizing Data

- Filtering Data

- Changing and Adding Data

- Summarizing and Grouping Data

There are still various purposes of SQL that you will encounter as you read this book, so read on.

Who can use SQL?

Anyone can use SQL, as long as the person knows the commands. Database programmers, website owners and application developers, however, use SQL widely to work on their huge databases.

For a beginner, like you, you can start using basic SQL commands in organizing your files, after you have read this book.

Chapter 2: Database Basics

Databases have typical attributes that you should know. Aside from containing organized files, they have also common parts that you must get acquainted with.

These are the usual parts of an access database.

1. **Tables**

    Tables are composed of columns and rows, with data that were usually normalized through the organization of the information. This prevents the redundancies of stored data.

    The columns are referred to as fields, while the rows are called records. Each of these items corresponds to different information in the database.

2. **Reports**

    Are summaries of the data or files from the database. They can be used to present tables of "total sales" within a month or within a year. They could also be used for printed reports or visual presentations. You can prepare formatted reports from your database of whatever summary information you may want to access.

3. Forms

Forms are the interfaces that you could use in accessing and managing your data. They are your ports of entry to your database hence they are also called data entry screens.

From your forms, you can enter commands to retrieve quickly, create, delete, add, or access a file or data.

Without your forms, it would be tedious for you to organize your databases because you have to go over your files individually.

From your forms, you can create commands that can protect your database. You can have ample control of your database such as, selecting files that only you can see, choosing files that the customer can view and protecting files that can't be viewed by the public.

On your forms, you could add other options and command buttons that you frequently use.

4. Modules

These are groups of commands and procedures that use the program, VBA (Virtual Basic for Applications), and are stored together in one unit.

There are two types of modules, the class and the standard modules. The class modules are those that are commonly attached to a specific data or file, while standard modules are found in the navigation panel.

Modules increase the functionality of your databases.

5. **Queries**

As previously discussed in chapter 1, there are various functions of queries (SQL) such as organizing and manipulating data. There are two types of queries, the select queries and the action queries.

The select queries have the function of selecting the data that you wish to work on, while the action queries have the function of helping you manipulate, organize, edit, add, or delete data.

All of these tasks can be displayed on your monitor or screen.

6. **Macros**

These are responsible for facilitating and automating your tasks when working on your databases. They provide a simplified programming language that you can use to edit your databases.

They are similar to the functions of modules because they increase the functionality of your databases.

7. **MySQL database server**

This is one of the SQL servers or software you can use to collect and manipulate your data. You can download MySQL for free to optimize your SQL learning experience.

Similar software programs are Microsoft SQL, IBM's DB2 and Oracle SQL.

8. Operators

Operators are words or characters that are used with the WHERE clause to perform certain operations such as, number operations, logical operations, comparisons and to negate conditions. They are discussed in detail in chapter 4.

9. Predicates

Used in SQL language to identify conditions, limiting the statements.

Chapter 3: SQL Syntax and SQL Queries

SQL has its own language elements, which is executed on a CLI (Command Line Interface). These are the necessary language commands that you can utilize for your databases. This language is your SQL syntax.

On the other hand, the SQL queries are used to search the databases for the data or files that you need.

It is important that you understand the basic language that is used for SQL queries to proceed successfully.

The SQL syntax is the basis of SQL queries, so at times, they are interchanged with one another.

SELECT STATEMENTS and SQL Queries

These SELECT STATEMENTS are not case-sensitive, but upper case letters are used in this book to facilitate reading. So, you can use lower case letters, if you want.

SQL queries can be more specific through the use of clauses such as ORDER BY (order by), FROM (from) and WHERE (where).

- ORDER BY - is a clause that refers to the sorting of the data;

- FROM - is the designated table for the search; and

- WHERE - is the clause that defines the rows specified for the query.

Take note of the following important SQL commands too. The terms are self-explanatory but for the sake of clarity, here they are:

- SELECT – This command extracts the file/data from your database.

- CREATE DATABASE – This command creates files/data.

- DELETE – This command erases file/data from your database.

- ALTER DATABASE – This command alters the file/data in your database.

- INSERT INTO – This command will allow you to insert a new file/data into your database.

- CREATE TABLE – You can also create a new table in your database with this command.

- DROP TABLE – This command is specifically used in deleting tables in your database.

- CREATE INDEX – You can create an index with this command. An index is the search key used for your database.

- DROP INDEX – With this command, you can drop or delete your index from your database.

IMPORTANT REMINDERS

SQL STATEMENTS (commands) are generally separated by a semicolon. But in a few, new database systems, reportedly, they don't make use of it. So, be aware of this.

The semicolon is used to separate SQL SELECT STATEMENTS, when there are more than one statements to be executed using the same server.

Below are examples of SELECT STATEMENTS or SQL Query

- SELECT "column_name2", "column_name3"

  FROM "table_name1"

  WHERE "column_name3"='value';

- SELECT * FROM

  WHERE "column_name"

  ORDER BY "column_name;

More keywords and SQL commands will be introduced as you read the book, so take it easy!

Chapter 4: Common Operators in SQL

As defined in chapter 2, operators are used with the WHERE clause to indicate the condition that you want to be performed in your tables.

You will need them to define the values in your tables.

Here are the most common operators with their corresponding symbols:

Comparison Operators

- Equal =

- Not equal <>

- Less than <

- Less than or equal <=

- Greater than >

- Greater than or equal >=

Logical operators

- **LIKE** - this keyword will allow you to retrieve the data that you will specify in your LIKE statement.

- **ALL** – this keyword is utilized to compare all values between tables.

- **BETWEEN** – this keyword displays range values within a set from the minimum to the maximum values. You can set the range of your values, using this keyword.

- **IS NULL** – this operator is used in the comparison of value to the NULL value in a set.

- **AND** – this operator is used to add more conditions in the WHERE clause of your SQL query.

- **IN** – this compares specified values in your tables.

- **OR** – this operator is also used with the WHERE clause to specify more conditions in a SQL query.

- **ANY** – this operator compares a value to any specified value indicated in the SQL statement.

- **EXISTS** – this operator or keyword searches for the specified condition in your SQL syntax.

- **UNIQUE** – this operator will allow the display of only unique values.

Arithmetic operators

- * The asterisk, when used as an arithmetic operator, will multiple values that are found before and after the symbol.

- + The plus sign will add the values that are positioned before and after the plus sign.

- / The division sign will divide the left value with the right value of the sign.

- - The minus sign will subtract the right value from the left value.

- % The percent sign divides the left value with the right value, and displays the remainder.

Learn how to use these operators properly to optimize your SQL statements and obtain tables that can be useful to you.

Chapter 5: Commonly Used Symbols in SQL

Before you can construct or create proper and correct SQL statements or queries, you have to know the most commonly used symbols in SQL.

SQL symbols

1. **Semicolon ;**

   This is used to end SQL statements or queries. It should always be added to complete the query. An exception is that of the Cache' SQL, which does not use semicolons.

2. **Open and close parentheses ( )**

   These have several uses. Those are used to enclose data types, conditions and sometimes names of columns. They are used also to enclose a subquery in the "from" clause, and arithmetic equations. In addition, when there are varied values and comma separated data.

3. **Double quotes " "**

   These indicate a delimited identifier or values.

4. **Singe quotes ' '**

This is used usually to enclose 'strings' of data types or conditions.

5. **Asterisk ***

The asterisk indicates "all" data, columns or tables.

6. **Underscore _**

This is used in table or column names to identify them properly. It is also used as an identifier.

7. **Percent %**

This is used as an identifier name for the first characters of your data such as, data names, system variables and keywords.

8. **Comma ,**

This symbol is used as a list separator such as, in a series of columns or multiple field names.

9. **Open and close square brackets [ ]**

This is used to enclose a list of match data types, or characters, or pattern strings.

10. **Plus +**

This is usually used in number operations.

You can read more of the symbols on "conditions" in chapter 9, step #5. There are still various symbols that you can learn as your knowledge advances.

These common symbols are appropriate for a beginner, who is just starting to learn SQL.

Chapter 6: How to Create Databases

As a beginner in SQL, you must know how to create DATABASES. Databases are simply systematic collections of data that can be stored in your computer, where they can be retrieved easily for future use.

The system is called DBMS (Database Management System), and is used extensively by all institutions that need to store large volumes of information or data.

Examples of data are: Name, Age, Address, Country, ID number and all vital information that have to be organized and stored.

The retrieval of these databases is possible through database software or programs such as, SQL, MySQL, ORACLE and other similar apps.

Creating databases is simple with this SQL statement:

Example: CREATE   DATABASE "database_name";

If you want to create a "MyStudents" database, you can state the SQL query this way:

Example: CREATE DATABASE MyStudents;

If you want to create a "My_Sales" database, you can state your SQL this way:

Example: CREATE DATABASE My_Sales;

The names of your databases must be unique within the RDBMS (Relational Database Management System). After creating your database, you can now create tables for your databases.

You can double check if your database exists by this SQL query:

Example: SHOW DATABASES;

This SQL statement will display all the databases that you have created.

It is important to note that your ability to retrieve or fetch the data that you have stored is one vital consideration.

Therefore, you have to choose the most applicable and most appropriate SQL server or software that you can optimize and synchronize with the computer you are using.

Chapter 7: Data Types

There are various data types that you should be familiar with. This is because they make use of SQL language that is significant in understanding SQL more.

There are six SQL data types

1. **Date and Time Data**

   As the name implies, this type of data deals with date and time.

   Examples are: DateTime (FROM Feb 1, 1816 TO July 2, 8796), small DateTime (FROM Feb 1, 2012 TO Mar 2085, date (Jun 1, 2016) and time (3:20 AM.).

2. **Exact Numeric Data**

   Under exact numeric data, there are several subtypes too such as;

   - *tinyint* – FROM 0 TO 255

   - *bit* – FROM 0 TO 1

   - bigint – FROM -9,223,372,036,854,775,808 TO 9,223,372,036,854,775,807

   - *numeric* – FROM $-10^{38}+1$ TO $10^{38}-1$

- *int* - FROM -2,147,483,648 TO 2,147,483,647

- *decimal* – FROM -10^38+1 TO 10^38-1

- *money* – FROM -922,337,203,685,477.5808 TO 922,337,203,685,477.5807

- *smallmoney* – FROM -214,748.3648 TO +214,748.3647

- *smallint* – FROM -32,768 TO 32,767

3. **Binary Data**

   Binary data have different types, as well. These are: Binary (fixed), varbinary (variable length binary) varbinary (max) (variable length binary) and image.

   They are classified according to the length of their bytes, with Binary having the shortest and the fixed value.

4. **Approximate Numeric Data**

   These have two types, the float and the real. The float has a value FROM - 1.79E +308 TO 1.79E +308, while the real data has a value FROM -3.40E +38 TO 3.40E +38

5. **Unicode Character Strings Data**

There are four types of Unicode Character Strings Data namely; ntext, nchar, nvarchar, and nvarchar (max). They are classified according to their character lengths.

For ntext, it has a maximum character length of 1,073,741,823, which is variable.

For nchar, it has a unicode maximum fixed length of 4,000 characters.

For nvarchar (max), it has a unicode variable maximum length of 231 characters.

For nvarchar, it has a variable maximum length of 4,000 unicode characters.

6. **Character Strings Data**

The character Strings Data have almost similar types as the Unicode Character Strings Data, only, some have different maximum values and they are non-unicode characters, as well.

For text, it has a maximum variable length of 2,147,483,647 non-unicode characters.

For char, it has a non-unicode maximum fixed length of 8,000 characters.

For varchar (max), it has a non-unicode variable maximum length of 231 characters.

For varchar, it has a variable maximum length of 8,000 non-unicode characters.

Miscellaneous Data

Aside from the 6 major types of data, miscellaneous data are also stored as tables, SQL variants, cursors, XML files, unique identifiers, cursors and/or timestamps.

You can refer to this chapter when you want to know about the maximum values of the data you are preparing.

Chapter 8: Downloading SQL Software

Although, almost all of the SQL queries presented here are general, it would be easy for you to adjust to whatever type of SQL server you will be using, eventually.

Before you can perform any SQL task in your computer, you have first to download a SQL software.

Since you're a beginner, you can use the free MySQL databases software. Hence, we will be focusing on how to download this application.

What is MySQL?

MySQL is a tool (database server) that uses SQL syntax to manage databases. It is an RDBMS (Relational Database Management System) that you can use to facilitate the manipulation of your databases.

If you are managing a website using MySQL, ascertain that the host of your website supports MySQL too.

Here's how you can install MySQL in your Microsoft Windows. We will be using Windows because it is the most common application used in computers.

How to install MySQL on Microsoft Windows in your computer.

Step #1 – Go to the MySQL website

Go to www.mysql.com and browse through the applications to select MySQL. Ascertain that you obtain the MySQL from its genuine website to prevent downloading viruses, which can be harmful to your computer.

Step #2 – Select the 'download' option

Next, click on the download option this will bring you to the MySQL Community Server, and to the MySQL Community Edition. Click 'download'.

Step #3 – Choose your Windows' processor version

Choose your Windows' processor version by perusing the details given on the page. Choose from the 'other downloads' label. You can choose the 32-bit or 64-bit.

Click the download button for the Windows (x86, 32-bit), ZIP Archive or the Windows (x86, 64-bit), ZIP Archive, whichever is applicable to your computer.

Step #4 – Register on the site

Before you can download your selected version, you will be requested to register by answering the sign in form for an Oracle account.

You don't have to reply to the questions that are optional. You can also click on the 'no thanks' button.

There is another option of just downloading the server without signing up, but you will not be enjoying some freebies such as, being able to download some white papers and technical information, faster access to MySQL downloads and other services.

Step #5 – Sign in to your MySQL account

After registering, you can sign in now to your new account. A new page will appear, select your area through the displayed images of flags. Afterwards, you can click the download button and save it on your computer.

This can take several minutes.

Step #6 – Name the downloaded file

After downloading the file. You can name your MySQL file and save it in your desktop or C drive. It's up to you, whichever you prefer.

Step #7 – Install your MySQL Server

Click the file to open it and then click 'install' to install MySQL on your computer. This will open a small window on your computer will ask if you want to open and install the program. Just click the "OK" button.

Step #8 – Browse your MySQL packages

The MySQL Enterprise Server page will appear giving you some information about what your MySQL package contains.

There are packages offered for a small fee, but since we're just interested in the community server, just click 'next' until you reached the 'finish' button.

Step #9 – Uncheck the box 'Register the MySQL Server now'

After the Wizard has completed the set-up, a box appears asking you to configure and register your MySQL Server. Uncheck the 'Register the MySQL Server now' box, and check the small box for the "Configure the MySQL Server now'.

Then click 'finish'.

Step #10 – Click 'next' on the Configuration Wizard box

A box will appear, and you just have to click next.

Step #11 – Select the configuration type

A box will appear, select your configuration type. Tick the small circle for the 'Detailed Configuration', instead of the 'Standard Configuration'. Click the 'next' button.

Step #12 – Select the server type

There will be three choices; the Developer Machine, the Server Machine and the Dedicated MySQL Server Machine.

Select the Server Machine because it will have medium memory usage, which is ideal for a beginner like you, who is interested to learn more about MySQL.

The Developer Machine uses minimal memory and may not allow you the maximum usage of your MySQL.

On the other hand, the MySQL Server Machine is for people who work as database programmers or full-time MySQL users. It will use all of the available memory in your computer, so it is not recommended for you.

Step #13 – Select the database usage

For database usage, there are three choices, namely; Multifunctional Database, Transactional Database Only, and Non-Transactional Database Only. Choose the Multifunctional Database because your purpose is for general purposes.

The Transactional and Non-transactional are used for more specific purposes.

Click the 'next' button at the bottom of the display box.

Step #14 – Select the drive for the InnoDB datafile

Or you can select the drive from your computer, where you want to store your InnoDB data file. Choose the drive you prefer and then click 'next'.

Step #15 - Set the number of concurrent connections to the server

This will indicate the number of users that will be connecting simultaneously to your server. The choices are; Discussion Support (DSS)/OLAP, Online Transaction Processing (OLTP) and Manual Setting.

It is recommended that you choose the option, DSS/OLAP because you will not be requiring a high number of concurrent connection. OLTP is needed for highly loaded servers, while the manual setting can be bothersome to be setting it every now and then.

After setting this, click 'next'.

Step #16 – Set the networking options

Enable the TCP/IP Networking by checking the small box before it. Below it, add your port number and then check the small box to Enable Strict Mode to set the server SQL mode.

Click 'next'.

Step #17 – Select the default character set

The most recommended is the Standard Character Set because it is suited for English and other West European languages. It is also the default for English.

The other two choices namely; Best Support For Multilingualism and the Manual Default Character Set are best for those who have other languages other than English.

Tick the small circle before the Standard Character Set and click 'next'.

Step #18 – Set the Windows options

Tick the two choices displayed, which are; Install As Windows Server and Include Bin Directory in Windows Path. This will allow you to work with your MySQL from your command line.

Selecting the Install As Windows Server will automatically display the Service Name. The small box below the Service Name must be checked too.

Click 'next'.

Step #19 – Set the security options

Set your password. The box will indicate where you can type it.

Click 'next'.

Step #20 - Execute your configurations

Click 'execute' and your computer will configure by itself based on your specifications.

Once the configuration is complete and all the boxes are checked, click 'finish'.

Step #21 – Set the verification process

- Type cmd and press enter in the start menu. This will take you to the command panel.

- Type the following:

  MySQL -u root -p

  Press 'enter'.

There is a space between MySQL and the dash symbol, and between u and root. Also, there is a space between the root and the dash symbol.

- The command panel will ask for your password. Type your password and press 'enter'.

- A MySQL prompt will appear.

- You can type any SQL command to display the databases. Add the semicolon at the end of your SQL statement.

- Close your command panel for the meantime.

Using your MySQL can motivate you to learn more about other related applications such as, PHP, and similar products.

What is important is for you to learn the basics of SQL first.

Chapter 9: How to Create Tables

Your tables are used to store the data or information in your database. They are composed of rows and columns as discussed in chapter 1. Specific names are assigned to the tables to identify them properly and to facilitate their manipulation. The rows of the tables contain the information for the columns.

Knowing how to create tables is important for a beginner, who wants to learn SQL.

The following are the simple steps:

Step #1 – Enter the keywords CREATE TABLE

These keywords will express your intention and direct what action you have in mind.

Example: CREATE TABLE

Step #2 – Enter the table name

Right after your CREATE TABLE keywords, add the table name. The table name should be specific and unique to allow easy and quick access later on.

Example: CREATE TABLE "table_name"

The name of your table must not be easy to guess by anyone. You can do this by including your initials and your birthdate. If your name is Henry Sheldon, and your birthdate is October 20, 1964, you can add that information to the name of your table.

Let's say you want your table to be about the traffic sources on your website, you can name the table "traffic_hs2064"

Take note that all SQL statements must end with a semicolon (;). All the data variables must be enclosed with quotation marks (" "), as well.

Example: CREATE TABLE traffic_hs2064

Step #3 – Add an open parenthesis in the next line

The parenthesis will indicate the introduction of the columns you want to create.

Example: CREATE TABLE "table_name"

(

Let's apply this step to our specific example.

Example: CREATE TABLE traffic_hs2064

(

In some instances, the parentheses are not used.

Step #4 – Add the first column name

This should be related to the data or information you want to collect for your table. Always separate your column definitions with a comma.

Example: CREATE TABLE "table_name"

("column_name"   "data type",

In our example, the focus of the table is on the traffic sources of your website. Hence, you can name the first column "country".

Example: CREATE TABLE traffic_hs2064

(country

Step #4 – Add more columns based on your data

You can add more columns if you need more data about your table. It's up to you. So, if you want to add four more columns, this is how your SQL statement would appear.

Example: CREATE TABLE "table_name"

("column_name1" "data type",

"column_name2" "data type",

"column_name3" "data type",

"column_name4" "data type");

Add the closing parenthesis and the semi-colon after the SQL statement.

Let's say you have decided to add for column 2 the keyword used in searching for your website, for column 3, the number of minutes that the visitor had spent on your website, and for column 4, the particular post that the person visited. This is how your SQL statement would appear.

Take note:

- The name of the table or column must start with a letter, then it can be followed by a number, an underscore, or another letter. It's preferable that the number of characters does not exceed 30.

- You can also use a VARCHAR (variable-length character) data type to help create the column.

- **Common data types are:**
    - **date** – date specified or value

    - **number (size)** – you should specify the maximum number of column digits inside the open and close parentheses

    - **char (size)** – you should specify the size of the fixed length inside the open and close parentheses.

    - **varchar (size)** – you should specify the maximum size inside the open and close parentheses. This is for variable lengths of the entries.

    - **Number (size, d)** – This is similar to number (size), except that 'd' represents the maximum number of digits.

        Hence if you want your column to show 10.21, your date type would be:

        number (2,2)

Example: CREATE TABLE traffic_hs2064

(country varchar (40),

keywords varchar (30),

time number (3),

post varchar (40));

Step #5 – Add CONSTRAINTS, if any

CONSTRAINTS are rules that are applied for a particular column. You can add CONSTRAINTS, if you wish. The most common CONSTRAINTS are:

- **"NOT NULL"** – this indicates that the columns should not contain blanks

- **"UNIQUE"** – this indicates that all entries added must be unique and not similar to any item on that particular column.

In summary, creating a table using a SQL statement will start with the CREATE TABLE, then the "table name", then an open parenthesis, then the "column names", the "data type", (add a comma after every column), then add any "CONSTRAINTS".

Add the closing parenthesis and the semicolon at the end of your SQL statement.

Chapter 10: Deleting Tables

Deleting tables, rows, or columns from your database is easy by using appropriate SQL statements. This is one of the commands that you must know to be able to optimize your introductory lessons to SQL.

Here are steps in deleting tables:

Step #1 – Select the DELETE command

On your monitor, choose the DELETE command and press the key. Downloading Window's MySQL Database, MySQL Connectors, and MySQL Workbench can facilitate your process.

Expert SQL users may laugh and say that these steps should not be included in this book. But for beginners, it is crucial to state specifically what steps should be done. Imagine yourself learning a totally new language; Russian, for example, and you'll know what I mean.

Step #2 – Indicate from what table

You can do this by adding the word "FROM" and the name of the table

> DELETE FROM 'table_name."

Make sure you select the proper table_name. Using our first sample example from the previous chapter, this is how your SQL statement would appear:

> Example: DELETE from traffic_hs2064

Step #3 – Indicate the specific column or row by adding "where."

If you don't indicate the "where" all your files would be deleted, so ensure that your statement is complete.

> Example: DELETE FROM 'table_name."
>
> WHERE "column_name"

Hence, if you want to delete the entire table, simply choose:

> DELETE FROM "table_name";

Using our previous example from chapter 1, this is how your SQL statement would appear:

Example: DELETE FROM traffic_hs2064

where time = (10)

DELETE   from
traffic_hs2064

where time = (5);

Step #4 – Complete your DELETE statement by adding the necessary variables

Example: DELETE FROM "table_name"

WHERE "column_name"

OPERATOR "value"

[AND/OR "column"

OPERATOR "value"];

Deleting the wrong tables from your database can cause problems, so, ascertain that you have entered the correct SQL statements.

Chapter 11: Inserting Data into a Table

You can insert new data into an existing table through the following steps.

Step #1 – Enter the keywords INSERT INTO

Select the keywords INSERT INTO. The most common program, which is compatible with SQL is windows MySQL. You can use this to insert data into your table.

Step #2 - Add the table name

Next, you can now add the table name. Be sure it is the correct table

Example: INSERT INTO "table_name."

Using our own table:

Example: INSERT INTO traffic_hs2064

Step #3 – Add Open parenthesis

You can now add your open parenthesis after the table name and before the column_names. Remember to add commas after each column.

Example: INSERT INTO "table_name."

(

Using our own table:

Example: INSERT INTO traffic_hs2064

(

Step #4 – Indicate the column

Indicate the column where you intend to insert your data.

Example: INSERT INTO "table_name."

("column _name", . . .
"column_name"

Step #5 – Close the columns with a close parenthesis

Don't forget to add your closing parenthesis. This will indicate that you have identified the columns accordingly.

Example: INSERT INTO "table_name."

("first_columnname", . . . "last_columnname")

Step #6 – Add the keyword values

The keyword values will help your selection be more specific. This is followed by the list of values. These values must be enclosed in parentheses too.

Example: INSERT INTO "table_name."

("first_columnname", . . . "last_columnname")

values (first_value, . . . last_value

Step #7 – Add the closing parenthesis

Remember to add the close parenthesis to your SQL statement. This will indicate that the column does not go any further.

Example: INSERT INTO "table_name."

("first_columnname", . . . "last_columnname")

values (first_value, . . . last_value)

Step #8 – Add your semicolon

All SQL statements end up with a semicolon, with the exception of a few.

Example: INSERT INTO "table_name."

("first_columnname", . . . "last_columnname")

values (first_value, . . . last_value);

Take note that strings must be enclosed in single quotation marks, while numbers are not.

Using our sample table, you can come up with this SQL statement:

Example: INSERT INTO "traffic_hs2064"

(country, keyword. time)

values ('America', 'marketing', 10);

You can insert more data safely without affecting the other tables. Just make sure you're using the correct SQL commands or statements.

Chapter 12: Dropping a Table

You can drop or delete a table with a few strokes on your keyboard. But before you decide to drop or delete a table, think about the extra time you may spend restoring it back, if you happen to need it later on. So, be careful with this command.

Dropping a table

Dropping a table is different from deleting the records/data in the table. When you drop a table, you are deleting the table definition plus the records/data in the table.

Example: DROP TABLE "table_name"

Using our table, the SQL statement would read like this.

Example: DROP TABLE traffic_hs2064;

Deleting data in a table

As discussed in the earlier chapters, this action will delete all the records/data in your table but will not delete the table itself. Hence, if your table structure is not removed, you can insert data later on.

The complete steps in deleting data or record in a table are discussed in another chapter.

DROPPING your table is easy as long as you can create the proper SQL.

Chapter 13: Selecting Data

Selecting a datum from your database can be done through the SELECT key. You only have to specify the data you want to select.

Step #1 – Choose the SELECT statement

Choose SELECT to identify your SQL command.

Step #2 – Choose the column

Choose the specific column where you want to retrieve the data.

Example: SELECT "column_name"

Step #3 – Use the asterisk * to select all columns

If you want to select all columns, use *, or you can also choose as many columns as you want.

Example: SELECT "column_name1"

["column_name2", "column_name3"]

Step #4 – Add FROM and the table name, where the data will come from

You can enclose the identified columns and where conditions with open and close square brackets [ ], but this is optional.

Example: SELECT "column_name"

["column_name", "column_name"]

FROM 'table_name"

WHERE "colum_name";

You can also write the above example in this way:

Example: select column_name, column_name, column_name

from table_name

where column_name;

Step #5 – Specify the "CONDITION"

You can specify the condition through the common operators that are presented in chapter 4.

Example #1: SELECT "column_name"

["column_name",
"column_name"]

FROM 'table_name"

[where   "colum_name"
"condition"];

You can also write the above example in this way: (no open and close square brackets)

Example   #2:   select   column_name,
column_name, column_name

from table_name

where   column_name
condition;

Example #3: SELECT "column_name"

[,   "column_name",
"column_name"]

FROM "table_name"

[WHERE "column_name"
LIKE 'Am'];

In the example above, all entries that start or match with 'Am' will be displayed.

> Example: SELECT "column_name"
>
> FROM "table_name"
>
> WHERE "column_name" = 'America';

In the example above, only the rows that exactly matches or equals 'America' will be selected.

Reminder:

You can remove the double quotes when using the actual names of the tables and columns.

Chapter 14: Sample SQL Queries

Before we proceed further, let's have some exercises for the simple SQL queries. A sample table is presented below to serve as your practice table.

Sample table Traffic_hs2064

> Traffic_hs2064

Country	Searchword	Time (minutes)	Post
America	perfect	5	Matchmaker
Italy	partner	2	NatureTripping
Sweden	mate	10	Fiction
Spain	couple	3	News
Malaysia	team	6	Health
Philippines	island	5	Entertainment
Africa	lover	4	Opinion

From the table above, construct or create your SQL statements, syntax or queries from the following instances.

1. Retrieve country, time and post only.

2. Retrieve country, searchword and post.

3. Retrieve all columns for every country that shows a time that is less than 5 minutes.

4. Retrieve all columns for every country that shows a time of more than 6 minutes.

5. Retrieve all columns for every country that contains 'America'.

6. Retrieve all files.

7. Retrieve all columns for every country that is not 'America'.

8. Retrieve searchword and post only.

9. Retrieve country and post only.

10. Retrieve all columns for every country, which name equals 'Italy'.

Try answering the exercises listed above on your computer, before looking at the answers. You can use a pencil and paper, so you can tweak your answers, if you feel more comfortable with this method.

Remember that your SQL command or key words (SELECT, DELETE, DROP TABLE, and similar statements) are not case sensitive, so you can use the lower case or upper case.

The column names and table names are not case sensitive in Microsoft but with UNIX, table names are case sensitive. You have to take note of the database software you are using.

When you retrieve the data, the results of your SQL query should, supposedly, be displayed on your monitor.

Here are answers; the SQL statements and the resulting tables (outputs)

1. SQL statement:

SELECT country, time, post FROM traffic_hs2064;

Resulting table

Traffic_hs2064

Country	Time (minutes)	Post
America	5	Matchmaker
Italy	2	NatureTripping
Sweden	10	Fiction
Spain	3	News
Malaysia	6	Health
Philippines	5	Entertainment
Africa	4	Opinion

2. SQL statement:

SELECT country, searchword, post FROM traffic_hs2064;

Resulting table

Traffic_hs2064

Country	Searchword	Post
America	perfect	Matchmaker
Italy	partner	NatureTripping
Sweden	mate	Fiction
Spain	couple	News
Malaysia	team	Health
Philippines	island	Entertainment
Africa	lover	Opinion

3. SQL statement:

SELECT country, searchword, time, post FROM traffic_hs2064

where time < 5;

or you could also state it this way:

SELECT * from traffic_hs2064 where time < 5;

Resulting table

Traffic_hs2064

Country	Searchword	Time (minutes)	Post
Italy	partner	2	NatureTripping
Spain	couple	3	News
Africa	lover	4	Opinion

4. SQL statement:

SELECT country, searchword, time, post FROM traffic_hs2064

WHERE time > 6;

or you could also express it this way:

SELECT * FROM traffic_hs2064 WHERE time > 6;

Resulting table

Traffic_hs2064

Country	Searchword	Time (minutes)	Post

Sweden	mate	10	Fiction

5. SQL statement:

SELECT * FROM traffic_hs2064

WHERE country = 'America';

Resulting table

Traffic_hs2064

Country	Searchword	Time (minutes)	Post
America	perfect	5	Matchmaker

6. SQL statement:

SELECT * FROM traffic_hs2064

Resulting table

Traffic_hs2064

Country	Searchword	Time (minutes)	Post
America	perfect	5	Matchmaker
Italy	partner	2	NatureTripping
Sweden	mate	10	Fiction
Spain	couple	3	News
Malaysia	team	6	Health
Philippines	island	5	Entertainment
Africa	lover	4	Opinion

7. SQL statement:

SELECT * FROM traffic_hs2064 WHERE country < > 'America';

Resulting table

Traffic_hs2064

Country	Searchword	Time (minute	Post

		s)	
Italy	partner	2	NatureTripping
Sweden	mate	10	Fiction
Spain	couple	3	News
Malaysia	team	6	Health
Philippines	island	5	Entertainment
Africa	lover	4	Opinion

8. SQL statement:

SELECT searchword, post FROM traffic_hs2064;

Traffic_hs2064

Searchword	Post
perfect	Matchmaker
partner	NatureTripping
mate	Fiction

couple	News
team	Health
island	Entertainment
lover	Opinion

9. SQL statement:

SELECT country, post FROM traffic_hs2064;

Resulting table

Traffic_hs2064

Country	Post
America	Matchmaker
Italy	NatureTripping
Sweden	Fiction
Spain	News
Malaysia	Health
Philippines	Entertainment
Africa	Opinion

10.SQL statement:

SELECT * FROM traffic_hs2064 WHERE country = 'Italy';

Resulting table

Traffic_hs2064

Country	Searchword	Time (minutes)	Post
Italy	partner	2	NatureTripping

These are basic SQL statements or queries that you must know before you can proceed to more complex forms.

Practice more with your own SQL software. Of course, by now, you should have downloaded an SQL program on your computer. Windows' MySQL program and Microsoft SQL server are more preferable for beginners.

Chapter 15: Combining and Joining Tables

There will be times that you have to combine tables. This task can be more complex than simply creating tables. But like everything that you do, the difficulty is all in your mind. If you think you can, then you can. So, here it goes.

The steps in combining tables are the following:

Step #1 – SELECT the columns you want to combine

You can indicate this with the SQL key word SELECT. This will display the columns you want to combine.

Example: SELECT "column_name", "colum_name" FROM "table_name"

Step #2 – Add the keyword UNION

Add the key word UNION to indicate your intent of combining the tables.

Example: SELECT "column_name", "column_name" from "table_name"

UNION

Step #3 – SELECT the other columns

Now, SELECT the other columns you want to combine with your first selected columns.

Example: SELECT "column_name", "column_name" FROM "table_name"

UNION SELECT "column_name", "column_name" FROM "table_name";

Step #4 – Use UNION ALL, in some cases

You can proceed to this step, in cases, when you want to include duplicate data. Without the key word "ALL", duplicate data would automatically be deleted.

Example: SELECT "column_name", "column_name" FROM "table_name"

UNION ALL SELECT "column_name", "column_name" FROM "table_name";

Combining tables with the SQL statement SELECT and JOIN

When your database server cannot handle the heavy load of your SELECT UNION query, you could also use the keyword JOIN.

The same steps apply for these statements. Add the appropriate JOIN keyword.

There are many types of JOIN SQL queries. These are:

- **INNER JOIN (SIMPLE JOIN)** – This will return or retrieve all data from tables that are joined. However, columns will not be displayed when one of the joined tables has no data.

  Example: SELECT "column1", "column2" FROM "table_name1"

  INNER JOIN "table_name2"

  ON   "table_name1".column"   = "table_name2.column";

  Let's say you have these two tables:

  Table A

  Students

Student No	LastName	FirstName	Age	Address	City
1	Potter	Michael	17	130 Reed Ave.	Cheyenne
2	Walker	Jean	18	110 Westlake	Cody
3	Anderson	Ted	18	22 Staten Sq.	Laramie
4	Dixon	Allan	18	12 Glenn Rd.	Casper
5	Cruise	Timothy	19	20 Reed Ave.	Cheyenne

Table B

StudentInformation

StudentNo	Year	Average
1	1st	90
2	1st	87
3	3rd	88
4	5th	77
5	2nd	93

You may want to extract specified data from both tables. Let's say from table A, you want to display LastName, FirstName and the City, while from Table B, you want to display the Average.

You can construct your SQL statement this way:

Example:

SELECT Students.LastName, Students.FirstName, StudentInformation.Average

FROM Students

INNER JOIN StudentInformation ON Students.StudentNo= StudentInformation.StudentNo;

This SQL query will display these data on your resulting table:

LastName	FirstName	Average
Potter	Michael	90
Walker	Jean	87
Anderson	Ted	88
Dixon	Allan	77
Cruise	Timothy	93

- **LEFT OUTER JOIN (LEFT JOIN)** – This SQL statement will display all rows from the left hand table (table 1), even if these do not match with the right hand table (table 2).

  With the ON key word, it will display only the rows specified. Data from the other table will only be displayed, if the data intersect with the first selected table.

  Example: SELECT "column1", "column2" from "table_name1"

  LEFT (OUTER) JOIN "table_name2"

  ON   "table_name1".column"   = "table_name2.column";

Let's use the two base tables above and create LEFT JOIN with the tables to display the LastName and the Year. You can create your SQL statement this way:

Example: SELECT   students.LastName, StudentInformation.Year

FROM students

LEFT JOIN StudentInformation

ON   Students.StudentNo   = StudentInformation.StudentNo;

Your resulting table will appear this way:

LastName	Year
Potter	1st
Walker	1st
Anderson	3rd
Dixon	5th
Cruise	2nd

- **RIGHT OUTER JOIN (RIGHT JOIN)** – This query will display all the rows from the right hand table (table 2). With the ON key word added, just like with the LEFT JOIN, it will display only the rows specified.

This SQL statement will display all data from table 2, even if there are no matches from table 1 (left table). Take note that only the data from table 1 that intersect with table 2 will be displayed.

Example: SELECT "column1", "column2" from "table_name1"

RIGHT (OUTER) JOIN "table_name2"

ON "table_name1".column" = "table_name2.column";

Let's use the same base tables above, to facilitate viewing, the two base tables are shown again on this page.

Table A

Students

Student No	LastName	FirstName	Age	Address	City
1	Potter	Michae	17	130	Cheye

		l		Reed Ave.	nne
2	Walker	Jean	18	110 Westlake	Cody
3	Anderson	Ted	18	22 Staten Sq.	Laramie
4	Dixon	Allan	18	12 Glenn Rd.	Casper
5	Cruise	Timothy	19	20 Reed Ave.	Cheyenne

Table B

StudentInformation

StudentNo	Year	Average
1	1st	90
2	1st	87
3	3rd	88
4	5th	77

5	2nd	93

And you want to perform a RIGHT OUTER JOIN or a RIGHT JOIN.

Here's how you can state your SQL query.

Example: SELECT Students.City, StudentInformation.Average

FROM Students

RIGHT JOIN StudentInformation

ON students.StudentNo = StudentInformation.StudentNo

ORDER BY Students.City;

Your result-table will appear like this:

City	Average
Cheyenne	90
Casper	77
Cheyenne	93
Cody	87
Laramie	88

- **FULL OUTER JOIN (FULL JOIN)** – This SQL keyword will display all the rows from both the left and right hand tables.

All data should be displayed by a query using these keywords. Take note that you should insert nulls when the conditions are not met in the joined tables

Example: SELECT "column1", "column2" from "table_name1"

FULL (OUTER) JOIN "table_name2"

ON "table_name1"."column" = "table_name2"."column";

Using the two base tables above, you can create your SQL FULL JOIN statement this way:

Example: SELECT Students.LastName, StudentInformation.Average

FROM Students

FULL JOIN StudentInformation

ON students.StudentNo = StudentInformation.StudentNo

ORDER BY Students.LastName;

This will be your table output:

LastName	Average
Potter	90
Anderson	93
Cruise	88
Dixon	87
Walker	77

There is no NULL VALUES in the columns because the column in both tables matched.

- **CROSS JOIN** – This SQL key word will display each row from table1 that combined with each row from table2.

  This is also called the CARTESIAN JOIN.

  Example: SELECT * from ["table_name1"] CROSS JOIN ["table_name2"];

Using the two base tables above, we can create a SQL statement this way:

Example: SELECT * from Students CROSS JOIN StudentInformation;

The output-table will be this:

StudentNo	LastName	FirstName	Age	Address	City	Year	Average
1	Potter	Michael	17	130 Reed Ave.	Cheyenne	1st	90
2	Walker	Jean	18	110 Westlake	Cody	1st	87
3	Anderson	Ted	18	22 Staten Sq.	Laramie	3rd	88
4	Dixon	Allan	18	12 Glenn Rd.	Casper	5th	77
5	Cruise	Timothy	19	20 Reed Ave.	Cheyenne	2nd	93

Making use of this JOIN SQL syntax properly can save time and money. Use them to your advantage.

Take note that when the WHERE clause is used, the CROSS JOIN becomes an INNER JOIN.

There is also one way of expressing your CROSS JOIN. The SQL can be created this way:

Example: SELECT LastName, FirstName, Age, Address, City

FROM Students

CROSS JOIN StudentInformation;

There will be slight variations in the SQL statements of other SQL servers, but the main syntax is typically basic.

Chapter 16: Pivoting Data

Pivoting data is converting your data, which are presented in rows, into column presentations.

Through the use of PIVOT queries, you can manipulate the rows and columns to present variations of the table that will help you in analyzing your table. PIVOT can present a column into multiple columns. You have also the option to use UNPIVOT query. UNPIVOT does the opposite of what PIVOT does.

It is extremely useful in multidimensional reporting. You may need it in generating your numerous reports.

How can you compose your PIVOT query?

Step #1 – Ascertain that your SQL can allow PIVOT queries

Is the version of your SQL server appropriate for PIVOT queries. If not, then you cannot accomplish these specific queries.

Step #2 - Determine what you want displayed in your results

Identify the column or data you want to appear in your results or output page.

Step #3 – Prepare your PIVOT query, using SQL

Use your knowledge of SQL to compose or create your PIVOT query.

To understand more about PIVOT, let's use the table below as a base table.

ProductSales

ProductName	Year	Earnings
RazorBlades1	2015	12000.00
BarHandles1	2016	15000.00
RazorBlades2	2015	10000.00
BarHandles2	2016	11000.00

Let's say you want an output that will show the ProductName as the column headings. This would be your PIVOT query:

Example #1:

SELECT * FROM ProductSales

PIVOT (SUM(Earnings)

FOR ProductNames IN ([RazorBlades1], [BarHandles1], [RazorBlades2], [BarHandles2]) AS PVT

With the PIVOT query above, your ProductSales table will now appear like this:

#ProductNamesPIVOTResults

Product Name	RazorBlades1	BarHandles1	RazorBlades2	BarHandles2
Year	2015	2016	2015	2016
Earnings	12000.00	15000.00	10000.00	11000.00

You can also manipulate the table based on your preferences.

Example #2

If you want the Year to be the column headings, you can write your PIVOT query this way:

SELECT * FROM ProductSales

PIVOT (SUM(EARNINGS)

FOR Year IN ([2015], [2016]) AS PVT

The resulting output would be the table below:

YearPivotResult

ProductName	2015	2016
RazorBlades1	12000.00	NULL
BarHandles1	15000.00	NULL
RazorBlades2	NULL	10000.00
BarHandles2	NULL	11000.00

There are more ways for you to use your PIVOT query.

For your UNPIVOT query, it will work the opposite way your PIVOT query does. It will convert the columns into rows.

Example

Using Exercise #1, you can come up with this UNPIVOT query:

SELECT ProductName, Year, Earnings

FROM #ProductNamesPivotResult

UNPIVOT (Earnings FOR ProductName IN ([RazorBlades1], [BarHandles1], [RazorBlades2], [BarHandles2]) AS UPVT

The output would be the original table:

#ProductSalesUnpivotResult

ProductName	Year	Earnings
RazorBlades1	2015	12000.00
BarHandles1	2016	15000.00
RazorBlades2	2015	10000.00
BarHandles2	2016	11000.00

Chapter 17: Updating Data

Updating or changing data is one task you must learn and engage in as a beginner SQL learner.

The key word for this SQL query is UPDATE. You can follow the steps below.

Step #1 – Create your UPDATE syntax

Prepare your update SQL query or syntax by using the keyword UPDATE.

Example: UPDATE "table_name"

SET   "column_name1"   =   value1, "column_name2"= value2;

Step #2 – Add the WHERE clause

Be sure to include the WHERE clause to identify the columns to be updated. Otherwise, all of your data will be updated.

Example: UPDATE "table_name"

SET "column_name1" = value1, "column_name2"= value2

WHERE some _"column_name"= some_value;

Step #3 – Double check your SQL syntax

You must double check your statement before clicking the enter button. One error can cause problems in your database.

Let's practice making UPDATE SQL statements from the table below. The table below is on "Online Students".

Students

Student No	LastName	FirstName	Age	Address	City
1	Potter	Michael	17	130 Reed Ave.	Cheyenne

2	Walker	Jean	18	110 Westlake	Cody
3	Anderson	Ted	18	22 Staten Sq.	Laramie
4	Dixon	Allan	18	12 Glenn Rd.	Casper
5	Cruise	Timothy	19	20 Reed Ave.	Cheyenne
6	Depp	Adam	17	276 Grand Ave.	Laramie
7	Lambert	David	19	32 8th St.	Cody
8	Cowell	Janine	18	140 Center St.	Casper
9	Kennedy	Daniel	17	11 21st St.	Laramie
10	Budzinak	Leila	20	24 Wing St.	Cheyenne

EXERCISE #1

Let's say you want to update or change the student "Walker, Jean" with a new address and city. How would you state your SQL query?

ANSWER:

Your SQL statement should appear this way:

Example: UPDATE students

SET Address = '34 Staten Sq', City = 'Laramie'

WHERE   LastName   = 'Walker';

REMINDER: AGAIN, Always indicate the WHERE clause to prevent updating all the data in your table.

If you have submitted the correct SQL query, your resulting table will appear like this:

Students

Student No	LastName	FirstName	Age	Address	City
1	Potter	Michael	17	130 Reed Ave.	Cheyenne
2	Walker	Jean	18	34 State n Sq.	Laramie
3	Anderson	Ted	18	22 State n Sq.	Laramie
4	Dixon	Allan	18	12 Glenn Rd.	Casper
5	Cruise	Timothy	19	20 Reed Ave.	Cheyenne
6	Depp	Adam	17	276 Grand Ave.	Laramie
7	Lambert	David	19	32 8th St.	Cody
8	Cowell	Janine	18	140 Center St.	Casper

9	Kenned y	Daniel	17	11 21st St.	Larami e
10	Budzin ak	Leila	20	24 Wing St.	Cheyen ne

EXERCISE #2

You want to update the address of Cowell, Janine to 20 18th St. Laramie City. What would your SQL syntax be?

Try creating your SQL statement without looking at the answer.

ANSWER:

UPDATE students

SET Address = '2018th St.', City = 'Laramie'

WHERE LastName = 'Budzinak';

If your SQL query is correct, your table will be updated according to your recent input.

Chapter 18: Filtering Data

Filtering data is an essential skill that you can learn as a beginner. There are various filtering activities that have been previously discussed in the past chapters by the use of the SQL keyword WHERE.

Filtering the data is similar to selecting the data you want to be displayed on your monitors.

WHERE indicates the content/file that can be found in your table.

Without the WHERE keyword, your SQL query would be 'lost in space' not knowing what data to filter and select.

You can use the following steps to filter your data.

Steps #1 – Decide what data to filter

Know specifically what date in your table you would like to filter. Once you have decided, go to the next step.

Steps #2 – Select the data

Write your SQL query with the keyword SELECT to indicate your selected data.

Make sure you have chosen properly. Inaccuracies in your query can produce wrong results.

You can write the SQL query like this:

Example: SELECT "column_name1, 'column_name2, "column_name3"

Remember to separate the column names with commas.

Using the table displayed below, compose your SQL query based on the stated premise.

Let's say you have chosen to filter all students below age 17, and want to display all students, who are older than 17.

How would you write your SQL statement?

Students

Student No	LastName	FirstName	Age	Address	City
1	Potter	Michael	17	130 Reed	Cheye

				Ave.	nne
2	Walker	Jean	18	110 Westlake	Cody
3	Anderson	Ted	18	22 Staten Sq.	Laramie
4	Dixon	Allan	18	12 Glenn Rd.	Casper
5	Cruise	Timothy	19	20 Reed Ave.	Cheyenne
6	Depp	Adam	17	276 Grand Ave.	Laramie
7	Lambert	David	19	32 8th St.	Cody
8	Cowell	Janine	18	140 Center St.	Casper
9	Kennedy	Daniel	17	11 21st St.	Laramie
10	Budzinak	Leila	20	24 Wing	Cheyenne

				St.	

You can write the SQL query like this:

> Example: SELECT LastName, FirstName, Address, City

Step #3 – Indicate FROM what table the data came from

After selecting the columns you want displayed, indicate FROM what table they should come from.

> Example: Example: SELECT LastName, FirstName, Address, City FROM Students

Step #4 – Add the WHERE clause

This is significant in filtering data, so remember to always use the WHERE clause. What data do you want to filter?

In the above exercise, you want to display all students above the age of 17. Hence, your resulting SQL statement would appear like this.

Example: SELECT LastName, FirstName, Address, City FROM students WHERE Age = > 17;

Step #5 – Always add the semicolon

SQL queries or statement almost always end with a semicolon. The semicolon is already added to the example above.

More examples and exercises will be given in the next chapters.

Chapter 19: Creating Indexes

Creating indexes is also essential knowledge that you should learn as a SQL beginner.

These indexes are essential when searching for data or tables because they provide an immediate and efficient result to queries.

To save time and effort, create indexes only for tables that you often use.

The basic CREATE INDEX SQL query is:

Example: CREATE INDEX "Index_name"

ON "table_name"; (you can include the "colum_name", if you   need that data)

Example: CREATE INDEX Studex

ON Students (Name, Age, City);

The SQL above will display all files - even duplicate files. If you want your result table to show only unique data, you can use the keywords CREATE UNIQUE INDEX, instead.

The basic SQL statement is similar with that of CREATE INDEX.

Here it is:

Example: CREATE UNIQUE INDEX "Index_name"

ON "table_name"; (you can include the "colum_name", if you   need that data)

Retrieve your tables quickly by using CREATE INDEX.

Chapter 20: Using the WHERE Clause

The use of the WHERE clause is crucial in creating SQL queries. Without the WHERE clause, some queries or statements cannot be completed. It is mostly used in filtering data, which is discussed in another chapter.

Here are the various functions of the WHERE clause:

1. It filters data. Columns that you have selected will be displayed in your output table.

   Example: SELECT   "column_name1", "column_name2", "column_name3"

   FROM "table_name"

   WHERE   "column_name"   operator value;

   Let's say this is your base table,

   BookSales

Name	Age	City	Book	Price
De Leon Dina	45	Canberra	Fiction	50.00
Danes Joan	24	Detroit	NonFiction	120.00
Lannister Ted	34	Grand Rapids	Fiction	60.00
Jahangiri Tom	43	San Antonio	Fiction	20.00
Mitchell Ben	29	Laramie	Fiction	30.00

And you want to display the columns for Name, City and Book only, you will be creating a SQL query in this manner:

Example: SELECT *

FROM BookSales

WHERE Book = 'Fiction';

Your resulting table (output) would appear this way:

BookSales

Name	Age	City	Book	Price
De Leon Dina	45	Canberra	Fiction	50.00
Lannister Ted	34	Grand Rapids	Fiction	60.00
Jahangiri Tom	43	San Antonio	Fiction	20.00
Mitchell Ben	29	Laramie	Fiction	30.00

Remember the * symbol, which indicates all column.

2. It can filter data for text fields versus numeric fields.

Example: SELECT *

FROM BookSales

WHERE Price <= 50;

Remember that numbers are not enclosed in single quotes, only letter strings are, such as, 'Canberra', 'Laramie'.

If you use the base table as your input table, the SQL syntax above will produce the table below.

BookSales

Name	Age	City	Book	Price
De Leon Dina	45	Canberra	Fiction	50.00
Jahangiri Tom	43	San Antonio	Fiction	20.00
Mitchell Ben	29	Laramie	Fiction	30.00

3. It can be used to retrieve or fetch data from your databases

Example: SELECT Name, Age, Book, Price

FROM BookSales

WHERE Age >20;

Using the base table and applying the SQL syntax with the WHERE clause, you will come up with this result table:

BookSales

Name	Age	Book	Price
De Leon Dina	45	Fiction	50.00
Danes Joan	24	NonFiction	120.00
Lannister Ted	34	Fiction	60.00
Jahangiri Tom	43	Fiction	20.00
Mitchell Ben	29	Fiction	30.00

4. **It can be used with character operators such as, LIKE, NOT, IN, and many more.** You can refer to chapters 27 & 33 for discussions on the most commonly used operators.

Example: SELECT *

FROM BookSales

WHERE Name LIKE d%;

The d% symbol indicates that you are selecting values in the name column that begin with the letter d. The % symbol denotes wildcards (missing letters). You can refer to chapter 21 for more information.

Based on the base table and the SQL statement in #4, your output table would be this:

BookSales

Name	Age	City	Book	Price
De Leon Dina	45	Canberra	Fiction	50.00
Danes Joan	24	Detroit	NonFiction	120.00

Here are more examples:

1. **Using the WHERE clause with the UPDATE keyword.**

   Example: UPDATE BookSales

   SET City = 'Canberra'

   WHERE Age = 24

Based on the original table, the resulting table would be this:

BookSales

Name	Age	City	Book	Price

De Leon Dina	45	Canberra	Fiction	50.00
Danes Joan	24	Canberra	NonFiction	120.00
Lannister Ted	34	Grand Rapids	Fiction	60.00
Jahangiri Tom	43	San Antonio	Fiction	20.00
Mitchell Ben	29	Laramie	Fiction	30.00

2. Using the WHERE clause with UPDATE

Example: UPDATE BookSales

SET Price=50

WHERE Name = 'Lannister Ted';

Using the base table to apply the SQL query to, this would be the resulting table.

BookSales

Name	Age	City	Book	Price
De Leon Dina	45	Canberra	Fiction	50.00

Danes Joan	24	Detroit	NonFiction	120.00
Lannister Ted	34	Grand Rapids	Fiction	50.00
Jahangiri Tom	43	San Antonio	Fiction	20.00
Mitchell Ben	29	Laramie	Fiction	30.00

Another example:

UPDATE BookSales

SET City = 'San Antonio', Age = 34

WHERE Names = 'Danes Joan';

The SET clause specifies what changes or updates you would like to do, while the WHERE clause identifies where you want those changes done. Hence with the SQL statement above, you want to UPDATE the data in your BookSales table by changing the City and Age entries on Danes Joan.

So, the resulting table will appear like this:

BookSales

Name	Age	City	Book	Price
De Leon Dina	45	Canberra	Fiction	50.00
Danes Joan	34	San Antonio	NonFiction	120.00
Lannister Ted	34	Grand Rapids	Fiction	60.00
Jahangiri Tom	43	San Antonio	Fiction	20.00
Mitchell Ben	29	Laramie	Fiction	30.00

The WHERE clause is essential in UPDATING your data because without it, all of your columns will be UPDATED with the same values.

The WHERE clause can be used in the AND and OR keywords such as, the example below:

Example: SELECT *

FROM BookSales

WHERE City = 'San Antonio'

AND Age >40;

Using the base table, your resulting table would be:

BookSales

Name	Age	City	Book	Price
Jahangiri Tom	43	San Antonio	Fiction	20.00

Example: SELECT *

FROM BookSales

WHERE City = 'Laramie'

OR City= 'Grand Rapids';

Using the base table, the resulting output would be this:

BookSales

Name	Age	City	Book	Price
Lannister Ted	34	Grand Rapids	Fiction	60.00
Mitchell Ben	29	Laramie	Fiction	30.00

Example: SELECT *

FROM BookSales

WHERE Book = 'Fiction'

AND (City = 'Laramie' OR City = 'Canberra');

Using the base table, the output table will appear this way:

BookSales

Name	Age	City	Book	Price
De Leon Dina	45	Canberra	Fiction	50.00
Mitchell Ben	29	Laramie	Fiction	30.00

There are more examples of the WHERE clause or keyword in the various chapters.

Chapter 21: Using TRANSACTIONS

A TRANSACTION is any task done against tables or files in a database. These transactions may range from simple to complex tasks, but whatever it is, you should ensure the reliability, integrity and credibility of your database.

Examples of transactions are; dropping, deleting, updating, joining tables, modifying and all the activities that you perform with your databases.

A single transaction may involve several tasks in one go.

That is why you have to know what to do in cases when there is system failure or there are aborted tasks.

There are commands that you must be familiar with if you want to protect your databases.

SAVEPOINT COMMAND

This command is used when you want to go back to some point in your transaction without the need to go back all the way to the very first activity. This will save time and effort.

The SQL statement for SAVEPOINT COMMAND is:

Example: SAVEPOINT SAVEPOINT_name;

ROLLBACK COMMAND

This command is useful when you would like to go back (roll back) to a point in the transaction that has not been saved yet in your database.

You cannot make another ROLLBACK COMMAND to a transaction that has already used the command.

The SQL statement for ROLLBACK COMMAND is:

Example: ROLLBACK;

As an example let's use the table below as our base table:

StudenInformation

StudentNo	Year	Average
1	1st	90
2	1st	87
3	3rd	88
4	5th	77
5	2nd	93
6	1st	88
7	1st	80
8	2nd	79
9	3rd	94
10	4th	80

Example: DELETE Average

FROM StudentInformation

WHERE StudentNo=5;

ROLLBACK;

Table-output is the same because of the ROLLBACK COMMAND:

StudentInformation

StudentNo	Year	Average
1	1st	90
2	1st	87
3	3rd	88
4	5th	77
5	2nd	93
6	1st	88
7	1st	80
8	2nd	79
9	3rd	94
10	4th	80

This SQL statement will first perform the first command, which is deleting the StudentNo with a value of 5, when you add the ROLLBACK COMMAND, the table will roll back to that point and will display the same results.

COMMIT COMMAND

The COMMIT COMMAND indicates that your transactions have been committed or saved to the database.

The SQL statement for the COMMIT COMMAND is simple:

Example: COMMIT;

Using the base table above, let's have specific examples.

Example: DELETE FROM Students

WHERE Average = 77;

COMMIT;

Based on the SQL query above and the original tables, the resulting table would look like this:

StudenInformation

StudentNo	Year	Average

1	1st	90
2	1st	87
3	3rd	88
5	2nd	93
6	1st	88
7	1st	80
8	2nd	79
9	3rd	94
10	4th	80

The row with a Grade = 77 was deleted and then COMMITTED (saved).

SET TRANSACTION COMMAND

The command is used to set the transaction that you have selected. The SQL statement for this SET TRANSACTION COMMAND is:

Example: SET TRANSACTION [read only];

Or

Example: SET TRANSACTION [read write];

RELEASE SAVEPOINT COMMAND

This command is used when you would like to remove a previous SAVEPOINT that you have created.

The SQL query for this command is:

Example: RELEASE SAVEPOINT SAVEPOINT_name;

Rolling back the transaction, after you have released the SAVEPOINT, is no longer possible. You have to perform the SQL according to the query on updating or modifying tables.

PROPERTIES OF TRANSACTIONS

There are certain PROPERTIES OF TRANSACTIONS that you should be aware of such as:

- **Consistency**

  This Indicates that the databases have changed consistently, after you have performed a transaction. If your database has an efficient DBMS, there will be no problem with the consistency of your transactions.

- **Durability**

  As the term implies, the data in your database remain 'durable' or unaltered in cases of system failure. They are durable like the branded Puma rubber shoes that many people wear. This is just to make a point.

- **Isolation**

  This indicates that transactions can function independently but, at the same time transparent. This is important when you want to work quicker and more efficiently.

- **Atomicity**

  Atomicity is one way by which the databases can protect themselves. This is because when there is task failure, it will abort the task and the transaction will ROLL BACK to its previous state. It ensures that all tasks within the transactions are done properly. This will ensure success in all the transactions that you have initiated.

You can transact successfully by using all the pointers above. You can do a quick read later when you encounter some problems with your SQL syntax.

Chapter 22: Using the TRUNCATE TABLE COMMAND

The TRUNCATE TABLE COMMAND is used when you want to delete data from a table that is already existing. This means you do not have plans of deleting the table, but only the contents.

While deleting the table can be quicker, it is not advisable because you might need the table format later on. Hence, TRUNCATING TABLE is the best option for you because the table is still there, enter the data once you have them.

The SQL statement for TRUNCATE TABLE is:

Example: TRUNCATE TABLE "table_name";

Using the base table in the previous chapter, which is, StudentInformation, you can now TRUNCATE this table with this SQL statement above.

StudenInformation

StudentNo	Year	Average
1	1st	90
2	1st	87
3	3rd	88
5	2nd	93
6	1st	88
7	1st	80
8	2nd	79
9	3rd	94
10	4th	80

Example: TRUNCATE TABLE StudentInformation;

This would be the result when you perform the SELECT keyword for the table.

Example: Empty set (0.00 sec)

Keep in mind that you can revive the table again and use it when you deem it appropriate.

Chapter 23: Using ORDER BY Clause

This chapter is focused on the use of the SQL key word ORDER BY. This clause is used to sort out the retrieved data or results displayed, after you have submitted your query.

It is a powerful keyword that can allow you to manipulate and edit the displayed results to suit your preferences.

The specific uses of the clause ORDER BY are the following:

1. **It can sort results in ascending order.**

    Example: SELECT "column_name"

    FROM "table_name"

    ORDER BY "column_name" ASC;

2. **It can sort results in descending order**

    Example: SELECT "column_name"

FROM "table_name"

ORDER BY "column_name" DESC;

3. It can sort several specified columns

Example: SELECT *

FROM "table_name"

ORDER BY "column_name1", "column_name2", "column_name3";

Using the table below, compose your SQL syntax that are specified.

Students

StudentNo	Names	Age	Address	City
1	Potter, Michael	17	130 Reed Ave.	Cheyenne
2	Walker, Jean	18	110 Westlake	Cody

3	Anderson, Ted	18	22 Staten Sq.	Laramie
4	Dixon, Allan	18	12 Glenn Rd.	Casper
5	Cruise, Timothy	19	20 Reed Ave.	Cheyenne
6	Depp, Adam	17	276 Grand Ave.	Laramie
7	Lambert, David	19	32 8th St.	Cody
8	Cowell, Janine	18	140 Center St.	Casper
9	Kennedy, Daniel	17	11 21st St.	Laramie
10	Budzinak, Leila	20	24 Wing St.	Cheyenne

EXERCISES

Compose the SQL statements for the following:

Exercise #1 - Sort the City in ascending order

Exercise #2 - Sort the Names in ascending order

Exercise #3 - Sort the Age from the youngest to the oldest student

Exercise #4 – Sort the Age from the oldest to the youngest student

Try composing your SQL statements before looking at the answers.

ANSWERS

Exercise #1

SELECT *

FROM Students

ORDER BY City ASC;

Using the base table, your resulting table will appear this way:

Students

StudentNo	Names	Age	Address	City
4	Dixon, Allan	18	12 Glenn Rd.	Casper
8	Cowell, Janine	18	140 Center St.	Casper
1	Potter, Michael	17	130 Reed Ave.	Cheyenne
5	Cruise, Timothy	19	20 Reed Ave.	Cheyenne
10	Budzinak, Leila	20	24 Wing St.	Cheyenne
2	Walker, Jean	18	110 Westlake	Cody
7	Lambert, David	19	32 8th St.	Cody
3	Anderson, Ted	18	22 Staten Sq.	Laramie
6	Depp, Adam	17	276 Grand Ave.	Laramie
9	Kennedy, Daniel	17	11 21st St.	Laramie

Exercise #2

SELECT *

FROM Students

ORDER BY Names DESC;

Using the base table, your resulting table will appear this way:

Students

StudentNo	Names	Age	Address	City
2	Walker, Jean	18	110 Westlake	Cody
1	Potter, Michael	17	130 Reed Ave.	Cheyenne
7	Lambert, David	19	32 8th St.	Cody
9	Kennedy, Daniel	17	11 21st St.	Laramie
4	Dixon, Allan	18	12 Glenn Rd.	Casper
6	Depp, Adam	17	276 Grand Ave.	Laramie
5	Cruise, Timothy	19	20 Reed Ave.	Cheyenne
8	Cowell, Janine	18	140 Center St.	Casper
10	Budzinak, Leila	20	24 Wing St.	Cheyenne
3	Anderson, Ted	18	22 Staten Sq.	Laramie

Exercise #3

SELECT *

FROM Students

ORDER BY Age ASC;

Using the base table, your output table will appear this way:

Students

StudentNo	Names	Age	Address	City
1	Potter, Michael	17	130 Reed Ave.	Cheyenne
9	Kennedy, Daniel	17	11 21st St.	Laramie
6	Depp, Adam	17	276 Grand Ave.	Laramie
2	Walker, Jean	18	110 Westlake	Cody
4	Dixon, Allan	18	12 Glenn Rd.	Casper
8	Cowell, Janine	18	140 Center St.	Casper
3	Anderson, Ted	18	22 Staten Sq.	Laramie
7	Lambert, David	19	32 8th St.	Cody
5	Cruise, Timothy	19	20 Reed Ave.	Cheyenne
10	Budzinak, Leila	20	24 Wing St.	Cheyenne

Exercise #4

```
SELECT *

FROM Students

ORDER BY Age DESC;
```

Using the base table, your resulting table will appear this way:

Students

StudentNo	Names	Age	Address	City
10	Budzinak, Leila	20	24 Wing St.	Cheyenne
7	Lambert, David	19	32 8th St.	Cody
5	Cruise, Timothy	19	20 Reed Ave.	Cheyenne
2	Walker, Jean	18	110 Westlake	Cody
4	Dixon, Allan	18	12 Glenn Rd.	Casper
8	Cowell, Janine	18	140 Center St.	Casper
3	Anderson, Ted	18	22 Staten Sq.	Laramie
1	Potter, Michael	17	130 Reed Ave.	Cheyenne
9	Kennedy, Daniel	17	11 21st St.	Laramie
6	Depp, Adam	17	276 Grand Ave.	Laramie

As you experience using the ORDER BY clause, you will surely enjoy creating your SQL statements.

Chapter 24: Using NULL VALUES

You can use the NULL VALUES whenever appropriate. The NULL values appear when the data are missing or unknown.

Hence, the default value in tables, where there are no DATA retrieved, is NULL. There are two types of NULL VALUES, the IS NULL and IS NOT NULL.

NULL VALUES are unlike numbers because they do not have a numerical value. A NULL VALUE is different from 0, so you cannot use the comparison operators namely, <, >, =, and so on, to test its value. Therefore, how can we determine the NULL VALUES?

Here's how:

Use, IS NULL and IS NOT NULL operators.

If the table below is your base table:

Students

StudentNo	Names	Age	Address	City
1	Potter,	17	130 Reed	Cheyenne

	Michael		Ave.	
2	Walker, Jean	18	110 Westlake	Cody
3	Anderson, Ted		22 Staten Sq.	Laramie
4	Dixon, Allan	18	12 Glenn Rd.	Casper
5	Cruise, Timothy	19	20 Reed Ave.	Cheyenne
6	Depp, Adam		276 Grand Ave.	Laramie
7	Lambert, David		32 8th St.	Cody
8	Cowell, Janine	18	140 Center St.	Casper
9	Kennedy, Daniel		11 21st St.	Laramie
10	Budzinak, Leila		24 Wing St.	Cheyenne

And you want to select all the NULL VALUES in the Age column, you can write your SQL query this way:

Example: SELECT Names, Age, Address, City

FROM Students

WHERE Age IS NULL;

Your SQL statement will retrieve the data with your result-table appearing like this:

Students

Names	Age	Address	City
Anderson, Ted		22 Staten Sq.	Laramie
Depp, Adam		276 Grand Ave.	Laramie
Lambert, David		32 8th St.	Cody
Kennedy, Daniel		11 21st St.	Laramie
Budzinak, Leila		24 Wing St.	Cheyenne

All the entries without values are retrieved or displayed together with the columns that you have specified.

Another example is this:

Example: SELECT *

FROM Students

WHERE Age IS NULL;

Using the base table, the output or resulting table will appear this way:

Students

StudentNo	Names	Age	Address	City
3	Anderson, Ted		22 Staten Sq.	Laramie
6	Depp, Adam		276 Grand Ave.	Laramie
7	Lambert, David		32 8th St.	Cody
9	Kennedy, Daniel		11 21st St.	Laramie
10	Budzinak, Leila		24 Wing St.	Cheyenne

Use IS NOT NULL

IS NOT NULL is used when you want to fetch the columns that have no NULL VALUES.

Your SQL syntax will be this:

Example: SELECT Names, Age, Address, City

FROM Students

WHERE Age IS NOT NULL;

Using the base table in this chapter, your resulting table would be:

Students

Names	Age	Address	City
Potter, Michael	17	130 Reed Ave.	Cheyenne
Walker, Jean	18	110 Westlake	Cody
Dixon, Allan	18	12 Glenn Rd.	Casper
Cruise, Timothy	19	20 Reed Ave.	Cheyenne
Cowell, Janine	18	140 Center St.	Casper

Another example is this:

Example: SELECT *

FROM Students

WHERE Age IS NOT NULL;

Using the base table, your output table will be:

Students

StudentNo	Names	Age	Address	City
1	Potter, Michael	17	130 Reed Ave.	Cheyenne
2	Walker, Jean	18	110 Westlake	Cody
4	Dixon, Allan	18	12 Glenn Rd.	Casper
5	Cruise, Timothy	19	20 Reed Ave.	Cheyenne
8	Cowell, Janine	18	140 Center St.	Casper

Take note that when you use the * sign, all the columns in the table are selected.

Chapter 25: Using NULL FUNCTIONS

Since you have learned about the IS NULL and IS NOT NULL values, you must also learn the NULL FUNCTIONS to maximize the use of the NULL VALUES.

There are four most common NULL FUNCTIONS. These are:

1. **IFNULL ()**

2. **ISNULL ()**

3. **NVL ()**

4. **COALESCE ()**

The function of each will be disclosed in the examples below.

We will use a new base table with the examples because the above-mentioned functions are useful in numerical tables.

BookSales

BookNo	Price	Sold	TotalSales

1	45.00	3	135.00
2	130.00	5	650.00
3	49.00	70	3430.00
4	60.00		
5	100.00		
6	75.00	50	3750.00
7	250.00	89	22250.00

In the table above, you have seen that there are some NULL VALUES. Some software may not be able to compute, if there are no specified values in some of the columns, so you have to add a value.

In the base table above, we can assign 0 as the value of NULL, so that we can fill in the blanks, leaving no blanks in the columns.

Here's how you can do it:

For MySQL

Example: SELECT   BookNo, Sold*(Price+IFNULL(TotalSales,0))

FROM BookSales;

This SQL query will result to this table:

BookSales

BookNo	Price	Sold	TotalSales
1	45.00	3	135.00
2	130.00	5	650.00
3	49.00	70	3430.00
4	60.00	0	0
5	100.00	0	0
6	75.00	50	3750.00
7	250.00	89	22250.00

The COALESCE () of MySQL can also be used this way:

Example: SELECT   BookNo, Sold*(Price+COALESCE(TotalSales,0))

FROM BookSales;

For MS (Microsoft) Access

In MS Access, there is a little difference in the SQL statement.

Example: SELECT BookNo,
Sold*(Price+IF(ISNULL(TotalSales),0,
(TotalSales));

FROM BookSales;

BookSales

BookNo	Price	Sold	TotalSales
1	45.00	3	135.00
2	130.00	5	650.00
3	49.00	70	3430.00
4	60.00	0	0
5	100.00	0	0
6	75.00	50	3750.00
7	250.00	89	22250.00

Basically the same table will result from the SQL query.

For ORACLE

We have to use the NVL () because the ISNULL function could not be performed. But the result-table is the same.

Example: SELECT BookNo,
Sold*(Price+NVL(TotalSales,0));

FROM BookSales;

This produces the same table with the SQL statement.

For SQL

SELECT BookNo,
Sold*(Price+ISNULL(TotalSales,0))

FROM BookSales;

This will also produce the same table as the other methods.

Chapter 26: Using the ALTER TABLE Query

There will be several times you need to use the ALTER TABLE command. This is when you need to edit, delete or modify tables and constraints.

The basic SQL statement for this query is:

Example: ALTER TABLE "table_name"

ADD "column_name" data type;

You can use this base table as your demo table:

Traffic_hs2064

Country	Searchword	Time	Post
America	perfect	5	Matchmaker
Italy	partner	2	NatureTripping
Sweden	mate	10	Fiction

Spain	couple	3	News
Malaysia	team	6	Health
Philippines	island	5	Entertainment
Africa	lover	4	Opinion

If your base table is the table above, and you want to add another column labeled City, you can create your SQL query this way:

Examples: ALTER TABLE Traffic_hs2064

ADD City char(30);

The output table would appear this way:

Traffic_hs2064

Country	Searchword	Time	Post	City

America	perfect	5	Matchmaker	NULL
Italy	partner	2	NatureTripping	NULL
Sweden	mate	10	Fiction	NULL
Spain	couple	3	News	NULL
Malaysia	team	6	Health	NULL
Philippines	island	5	Entertainment	NULL
Africa	lover	4	Opinion	NULL

You can also ALTER a table to ADD a constraint such as, NOT NULL.

Example: ALTER TABLE Traffic_hs2064

MODIFY City datatype NOT NULL;

This will modify all entries that are NOT NULL.

You can also ALTER TABLE to DROP COLUMNS such as, the example below:

Example: ALTER TABLE Traffic_hs2064 DROP COLUMN Time;

Using the second table with this SQL query, the resulting table will be this:

Traffic_hs2064

Country	Searchword	Post	City
America	perfect	Matchmaker	NULL
Italy	partner	NatureTripping	NULL
Sweden	mate	Fiction	NULL

Spain	couple	News	NULL
Malaysia	team	Health	NULL
Philippines	island	Entertainment	NULL
Africa	lover	Opinion	NULL

You can ALTER TABLE by adding a UNIQUE CONSTRAINT. You can construct your SQL query this way:

Example: ALTER TABLE Traffic_hs2064

ADD CONSTRAINT uc_Country UNIQUE (Country, SearchWord);

In addition to these uses, the ALTER TABLE can also be used with the DROP CONSTRAINT like the example below.

Example: ALTER TABLE Traffic_hs2064

DROP CONSTRAINT uc_City;

Here are examples of CONSTRAINTS.

- **NOT NULL**

  This constraint indicates that the NOT NULL values should not be present in the columns of a stored table.

- **CHECK**

  This will ensure that all parameters have values that have met the criteria.

- **UNIQUE**

  This ascertains that all values in the columns are distinct or unique.

- **PRIMARY KEY**

  This indicates that the values in two or more columns are NOT NULL and simultaneously UNIQUE.

- **FOREIGN KEY**

  This will ascertain that the values of columns from different tables match.

- **DEFAULT**

There is a specified DEFAULT value for columns. This may appear as blanks or appear as NULL.

Make sure you use these constraints properly to make the most out of your SQL queries.

Chapter 27: Using BETWEEN Operator

The BETWEEN operator is usually used with numbers and dates, when you want to choose values within a certain range. Texts can also use the operator, BETWEEN.

The results displayed by a BETWEEN operator, can vary for different databases. In some databases, the selected columns may include the first value and the second value in its output, while some databases will exclude them.

There may also be a possibility when the first value is included in the output table, but not the second value specified. You may want to double check the outputs before finalizing your tables.

The BETWEEN operator can be used in a SQL query in the following manner.

Example: SELECT "column_name" (can be many columns)

FROM "table_name"

WHERE "column_name" BETWEEN "value1" AND "value2";

You can also write the SQL query this way, if you want to include all the columns.

Example: SELECT *

FROM "table_name"

WHERE "column_name" BETWEEN "value1" AND "value2";

Using the sample table below on Employees_Salary, compose your BETWEEN SQL syntax.

Employees_Salary

Names	Age	Salary	City
Williams, Michael	22	30000.00	Casper
Colton, Jean	24	37000.00	San Diego

Anderson, Ted	30	45000.00	Laramie
Dixon, Allan	27	43000.00	Chicago
Clarkson, Tim	25	35000.00	New York
Alaina, Ann	32	41000.00	Ottawa
Rogers, David	29	50000.00	San Francisco
Lambert, Jancy	38	47000.00	Los Angeles
Kennedy, Tom	27	34000.00	Denver
Schultz, Diana	40	46000.00	New York

Example: SELECT *

FROM Employees_Salary

WHERE Age BETWEEN 22 AND 30;

The SQL statement above will produce this table:

Employees_Salary

Names	Age	Salary	City
Williams, Michael	22	30000.00	Casper
Colton, Jean	24	37000.00	San Diego

Anderson, Ted	30	45000.00	Laramie
Dixon, Allan	27	43000.00	Chicago
Clarkson, Tim	25	35000.00	New York
Rogers, David	29	50000.00	San Francisco
Kennedy, Tom	27	34000.00	Denver

Another version of the BETWEEN operator is the NOT BETWEEN.

This SQL keyword will display the content of the table that are outside the range of the specified values.

Example: SELECT *

FROM Employees_Salary

WHERE Age NOT BETWEEN 22 AND 30;

The output of the SQL statement above is the table below:

Employees_Salary

Names	Age	Salary	City
Alaina, Ann	32	41000.00	Ottawa
Lambert, Jancy	38	47000.00	Los Angeles
Schultz, Diana	40	46000.00	New York

The SQL keywords BETWEEN and NOT BETWEEN are essential especially for numbers.

Know how to use the BETWEEN operator well to create your tables.

However, take note that these keywords can also be used with text values.

For this SQL queries, the sample table is this.

Employees_Salary

Names	Age	Salary	City
Williams, Michael	22	30000.00	Casper
Colton, Jean	24	37000.00	San Diego
Anderson, Ted	30	45000.00	Laramie
Dixon, Allan	27	43000.00	Chicago
Clarkson, Tim	25	35000.00	New York
Alaina, Ann	32	41000.00	Ottawa
Rogers, David	29	50000.00	San Francisco
Lambert, Jancy	38	47000.00	Los Angeles
Kennedy, Tom	27	34000.00	Denver
Schultz, Diana	40	46000.00	New York

Let's say you want your output or result table to display all cities beginning with any of the letters between 'B' and 'D', you can express your SQL statement this way.

Example: SELECT *

FROM Employees_Salary

WHERE City BETWEEN 'B' AND 'D';

Your result or output from the SQL query above will be the table below.

Employees_Salary

Names	Age	Salary	City
Williams, Michael	22	30000.00	Casper
Dixon, Allan	27	43000.00	Chicago
Kennedy, Tom	27	34000.00	Denver

For the use of the NOT BETWEEN keyword or operator, you can follow the same statement with the number values.

Example: SELECT *

FROM Employees_Salary

WHERE   City   NOT
BETWEEN 'B' AND 'D';

Remember to enclose your letters within single quotes. This is important to make your SQL query complete.

If you use the same original table above, your output with the SQL syntax would be the table below.

Employees_Salary

Names	Age	Salary	City
Colton, Jean	24	37000.00	San Diego
Anderson, Ted	30	45000.00	Laramie
Clarkson, Tim	25	35000.00	New York
Alaina, Ann	32	41000.00	Ottawa
Rogers, David	29	50000.00	San Francisco
Lambert, Jancy	38	47000.00	Los Angeles
Schultz, Diana	40	46000.00	New York

You can also use BETWEEN with IN to exclude certain entries that you don't want to display.

From the sample table below:

Employees_Salary

Names	Age	Salary	City
Williams, Michael	22	30000.00	Casper
Colton, Jean	24	37000.00	San Diego
Anderson, Ted	30	45000.00	Laramie
Dixon, Allan	27	43000.00	Chicago
Clarkson, Tim	25	35000.00	New York
Alaina, Ann	32	41000.00	Ottawa
Rogers, David	29	50000.00	San Francisco
Lambert, Jancy	38	47000.00	Los Angeles
Kennedy, Tom	27	34000.00	Denver
Schultz, Diana	40	46000.00	New York

Let's say you want to display in your output table all the cities with any of the letters between 'B' and 'D', but not those who are aged 22, 23 and 24.

This is how you express your SQL statement;

Example: SELECT *

FROM Employees_Salary

WHERE (City BETWEEN 'B' AND 'D')

AND NOT Age IN (22, 23,24);

Your output or result would be the table below:

Employees_Salary

Names	Age	Salary	City
Anderson, Ted	30	45000.00	Laramie
Clarkson, Tim	25	35000.00	New York
Alaina, Ann	32	41000.00	Ottawa
Rogers, David	29	50000.00	San Francisco

Lambert, Jancy	38	47000.00	Los Angeles
Schultz, Diana	40	46000.00	New York

You can also use the BETWEEN operator with date values. Your sample table is:

Employees_Salary

Names	Age	Salary	City	DateOfEntry
Colton, Jean	24	37000.00	San Diego	8/21/2015
Anderson, Ted	30	45000.00	Laramie	10/5/2014
Clarkson, Tim	25	35000.00	New York	6/6/2012
Alaina, Ann	32	41000.00	Ottawa	7/20/2010
Rogers, David	29	50000.00	San Francisco	9/25/2014
Lambert, Jancy	38	47000.00	Los Angeles	10/20/2013

Schultz, Diana	40	46000.00	New York	3/5/2016

Here is an example:

Example: SELECT *

      FROM Employees_Salary

      WHERE DateOfEntry BETWEEN #07/20/2010# AND #06/20/2012#;

This SQL query will display the table below:

Employees_Salary

Names	Age	Salary	City	DateOfEntry
Clarkson, Tim	25	35000.00	New York	6/6/2012
Alaina,	32	41000.00	Ottaw	7/20/2010

Ann			a	

The BETWEEN clause is crucial, especially for numerical values, so remember to use this significant clause in your SQL statements.

Chapter 28: Using AND and OR

The AND and OR operators are important in SQL because they are used to create complex SQLs and to filter data based on one or more conditions.

To be more accurate, the AND operator is used when you want to display data or file that are true with both specified conditions.

On the other hand, the OR operator works the other way around, the keyword will display either of the specified data, record or file.

Using AND

Let's say your base or original table is this:

Employees_Salary

Names	Age	Salary	City	DateOfEntry
Colton, Jean	24	37000.00	San Diego	8/21/2015

Anderson, Ted	30	45000.00	Laramie	10/5/2014
Clarkson, Tim	25	35000.00	New York	6/6/2012
Alaina, Ann	32	41000.00	Ottawa	7/20/2010
Rogers, David	29	50000.00	San Francisco	9/25/2014
Lambert, Jancy	38	47000.00	Los Angeles	10/20/2013
Schultz, Diana	40	46000.00	New York	3/5/2016

And you want your resulting table to display both the Age of those below 30 and those who live in New York, your SQL query would be:

Example: SELECT *

FROM Employees_Salary

WHERE Age = < 30

AND City = 'New York';

Employees_Salary

Names	Age	Salary	City	DateOfEntry
Clarkson, Tim	25	35000.00	New York	6/6/2012

Using OR

With the same base table above, create an SQL making use of the same parameter/files, but using the OR operator.

Example: SELECT *

FROM Employees_Salary

WHERE City = 'New York'

OR City = "San Diego';

The resulting table or data output would be the table below.

Employees_Salary

Names	Age	Salary	City	DateOfEntry
Colton, Jean	24	37000.00	San Diego	8/21/2015

Clarkson, Tim	25	35000.00	New York	6/6/2012
Schultz, Diana	40	46000.00	New York	3/5/2016

Combining AND and OR operators

Combining your AND and OR operators can help you create more tables according to your preferences. Remember to use the parenthesis in complex SQL statements or expressions.

These are examples on how to use your AND and OR operators. Try some of these exercises.

Base table

Employees_Salary

Names	Age	Salary	City	DateOfEntry
Colton, Jean	24	37000.00	San Diego	8/21/2015
Anderson, Ted	30	45000.00	Laramie	10/5/2014

Clarkson, Tim	25	35000.00	New York	6/6/2012
Alaina, Ann	32	41000.00	Ottawa	7/20/2010
Rogers, David	29	50000.00	San Francisco	9/25/2014
Lambert, Jancy	38	47000.00	Los Angeles	10/20/2013
Schultz, Diana	40	46000.00	New York	3/5/2016

Example: SELECT * FROM Employees_Salary

WHERE City = 'San Diego'

AND (Age = 24 OR Age = 26);

Your output or resulting table would appear like this:

Employees_Salary

Names	Age	Salary	City	DateOfEntry

Colton, Jean	24	37000.00	San Diego	8/21/2015

Learn more in using your AND and OR operators by doing some exercises with your own tables.

There are more examples given in the chapter for the WHERE clause.

Chapter 29: Using SELECT DISTINCT Query

Another SQL keyword that you should know is the SELECT DISTINCT statement.

There is a difference between a SELECT statement from a SELECT DISTINCT statement or query.

The SELECT statement will display all files even if there are similar contents, while the SELECT DISTINCT statement will only display values or content that are unique, different or distinct.

This the basic SELECT DISTINCT query.

Example: SELECT   DISTINCT
"column_name1",   "column_name2",
"column_name3"

FROM "table_name";

If you have the table below:

Online_Students

Name	Age	City	Country
Pollack,	25	Anchorage	United

Leni			States
Cooper, Brian	18	Atlanta	United States
Urban, Ned	56	Manila	Philippines
Lowell, Cathy	45	Madrid	Spain
Moore, Virginia	18	Seoul	South Korea

And you want to display DISTINCT values of Age from your Online_Students table, you can express your SQL query this way:

Example: SELECT DISTINCT Age from Online_Students;

Your resulting table would appear this way. There are two 18 entries, so only one entry appears, and the duplicate entry is excluded.

Online_Students

Age
18

25
56
45

You may want to include the names, so you express your SQL query this way:

Example: SELECT DISTINCT Name, City

FROM Online_Students;

Your resulting table or output would be this table, since all the entries are DISTINCT, your values will all appear in your output.

Online_Students

Name	City
Pollack, Leni	Anchorage
Cooper, Brian	Atlanta
Urban, Ned	Manila
Lowell, Cathy	Madrid
Moore, Virginia	Seoul

If you want to SELECT DISTINCT Name and Age from the same table, your SQL query would read:

Example: SELECT DISTINCT Name, Age

FROM Online_students;

Your resulting table would be:

Online_Students

Name	Age
Pollack, Leni	25
Cooper, Brian	18
Urban, Ned	56
Lowell, Cathy	45
Moore, Virginia	18

Take note that in the Age column, there are two Age 18 entries, but they are both displayed or retrieved on the new table because both their Names are DISTINCT.

Just remember that the DISTINCT keyword or statement removes duplicates on the specified columns.

Chapter 30: Using SELECT TOP

The use of SELECT TOP in SQL statements cannot be discounted due to the fact that it is very useful to retrieve a number of data from thousands of tables in the database.

There are slight differences in the SQL query, depending on the server used.

MySQL statement

You can create the basic SELECT TOP MySQL statement this way:

Example: SELECT "column_name1", "column_name2", ...

FROM "table_name"

LIMIT number;

MS Access Statement

Usually, the basic SQL statement for MS Access is:

Example: SELECT TOP number/percent "column_name1", "column_name2", "column_name3", ...

FROM "table_name";

If your table is the table below:

Online_Students

Name	Age	City	Country
Pollack, Leni	25	Anchorage	United States
Cooper, Brian	18	Atlanta	United States
Urban, Ned	56	Manila	Philippines
Lowell, Cathy	45	Madrid	Spain
Moore, Virginia	18	Seoul	South Korea

And you want to the SELECT TOP 2, your SQL statement would be:

Example: SELECT TOP 2

FROM Online_Students;

The output would be the table below:

Online_Students

Name	Age	City	Country
Pollack, Leni	25	Anchorage	United States
Cooper, Brian	18	Atlanta	United States

ORACLE statement

Example: SELECT "column_name1" (you may add other columns)

FROM "table_name"

WHERE ROWNUM <= number;

Using the base table above, you can create your ORACLE statement this way:

Example: SELECT *

FROM   Online_Students

WHERE ROWNUM <= 4;

Using the base table in this chapter, the resulting table will appear this way:

Online_Students

Name	Age	City	Country
Pollack, Leni	25	Anchorage	United States
Cooper, Brian	18	Atlanta	United States
Urban, Ned	56	Manila	Philippines
Lowell, Cathy	45	Madrid	Spain

The output table is the above table, since the value indicated is <=4.

This means that the ROWNUM (ROW NUMBER) is equal or less than 4.

Sometimes, the ROWNUM is used together with the ORDER BY clause:

Example: SELECT *

FROM   Online_Students

WHERE ROWNUM <= 4

ORDER BY Name;

Using the base table, the resulting table is this. The Names were arranged first, and then the ROWNUM <=4 is applied.

Online_Students

Name	Age	City	Country
Cooper, Brian	18	Atlanta	United States
Lowell, Cathy	45	Madrid	Spain
Moore, Virginia	18	Seoul	South Korea
Pollack, Leni	25	Anchorage	United States

The ROWNUM is often used in ORACLE.

The WHERE and ORDER BY clause can be interchanged in their positions in the SQL query. You will have to try both to see what comes out with the best results depending on the type of table you need.

Chapter 31: Using the LIKE Clause and WILDCARDS

The LIKE statement in SQL is typically used with WILDCARD operators. The use of the LIKE keyword is to compare a value or data with similar values.

The LIKE clause usually makes use of two WILDCARD operators namely: the underscore "_" and the percent (%) symbols.

The underscore indicates a single character or number, while the percent sign indicates several numbers or characters.

Here's an example of a basic SQL making use of LIKE and the WILDCARDS.

Example: SELECT FROM "table_name"

WHERE "column_name" LIKE '%value%' (or value%)

Example: SELECT FROM "table_name"

WHERE "column_name" LIKE 'value_' (or value_, or _value)

Take note that the value can be a number or a string. Also, depending on the table that you need, you can indicate whether the value that you want is found at the beginning, middle or end of the values.

Here are examples:

The SQL statements below are all based on this base table or demo table:

Employees_Salary

Names	Age	Salary	City
Williams, Michael	22	30000.00	Casper
Colton, Jean	24	37000.00	San Diego
Anderson, Ted	30	45000.00	Laramie
Dixon, Allan	27	43000.00	Chicago
Clarkson, Tim	25	35000.00	New York
Rogers, David	29	50000.00	San Francisco
Kennedy, Tom	27	34000.00	Denver

If you want to manipulate the data of the table above to compare the values in the Salary column, you can write your SQL statement this way:

Example: SELECT   FROM Employees_Salary

WHERE   Salary   LIKE '%300%';

The above SQL query will display any Salary, where 300 is found in any position.

Applying the above query, the table output would be:

Employees_Salary

Names	Age	Salary	City
Williams, Michael	22	30000.00	Casper
Dixon, Allan	27	43000.00	Chicago

Example: SELECT FROM Employess_Salary

WHERE Salary LIKE '300%';

The position of the value (coming before the % sign) indicates that all Salaries starting with 300 will be displayed.

Using the base table above, the resulting table would be like this:

Employees_Salary

Names	Age	Salary	City
Williams, Michael	22	30000.00	Casper

Example: SELECT   FROM Employees_Salary

WHERE Salary LIKE '4_ _ _ 0';

This SQL statement denotes that the Salary you want displayed in your resulting table are those that start with 4 and will end with 0; all must be 5-digit numbers.

Using the base table, your resulting table would be:

Employees_Salary

Names	Age	Salary	City
Anderson, Ted	30	45000.00	Laramie
Dixon, Allan	27	43000.00	Chicago

Example: SELECT FROM Employees_Salary

WHERE Salary LIKE '%00';

The SQL query indicates that any value that ends with 00 will be displayed on the resulting table.

Employees_Salary

Names	Age	Salary	City
Williams, Michael	22	30000.00	Casper
Colton, Jean	24	37000.00	San Diego
Anderson, Ted	30	45000.00	Laramie
Dixon, Allan	27	43000.00	Chicago
Clarkson, Tim	25	35000.00	New York
Rogers, David	29	50000.00	San Francisco

Kennedy, Tom	27	34000.00	Denver

Since all the Salaries end with oo, they are all included in the output.

Example: SELECT FROM Employees_Salary

WHERE Salary LIKE '3_%_%_%_%';

The above SQL statement means that all values starting with 3 is followed by non-specified 4 more succeeding values. This will have to be a 5 digit number displayed on the resulting table.

Employees_Salary

Names	Age	Salary	City
Williams, Michael	22	30000.00	Casper
Colton, Jean	24	37000.00	San Diego
Clarkson, Tim	25	35000.00	New York
Kennedy, Tom	27	34000.00	Denver

Example: SELECT FROM Employees_Salary

WHERE Salary LIKE '_oo';

This SQL query is retrieving the values in the Salary column that have oo in the second and third positions.

Hence, the resulting table will be this:

Employees_Salary

Names	Age	Salary	City
Williams, Michael	22	30000.00	Casper
Rogers, David	29	50000.00	San Francisco

Example: SELECT FROM Employees_Salary

WHERE Salary LIKE '_3%0';

This means that you want your output table to display values that have 3 in the second position and 0 at the end.

This will result to the table below:

Employees_Salary

Names	Age	Salary	City
Dixon, Allan	27	43000.00	Chicago

Isn't it amazing that you can modify the number data in your columns so easily with the use of SQL?

You can practice more to retain the information fully in your mind.

Chapter 32: Using ALIASES

Sometimes you need to rename a table to facilitate your SQL query. This renamed table are termed ALIASES.

They are only temporary and do not change the name of your base table in your databases.

ALIASES are useful when your SQL query uses more than one table; when you want to combine columns; when your column_names are long or vague, and you want to change them for something simpler and more precise.

You can also use ALIASES when you want to define the functions in your SQL statement.

Here is an example; SQL query using ALIASES:

For tables:

Example: SELECT   "column_name1, "column_name2"

FROM "table_name" AS "alias_name"

WHERE [condition];

For columns:

Example: SELECT "column_name" AS "alias_name"

FROM "table_name"

WHERE [condition];

If these are your tables:

Table A

EnrolledStudents

IDNo	LastName	FirstName	Age
00100	Slater	Christian	21
00200	Lannister	Kerry	20
00300	Hall	Lenny	22

00400	Daniels	Willy	20
00500	Hanson	Gilbert	23

Table B

StudentsCourse

IDNo	Course	Year
00100	BSMT	1st
00200	BSBA	2nd year
00300	BSEd	1st year
00400	BSMT	3rd year
00500	BSPT	4th year

You want to create an ALIAS for your columns, you can do it this way:

Example: SELECT LastName AS Last, FirstName AS first

FROM EnrolledStudents;

Your table output would be this:

EnrolledStudents

IDNo	Last	First	Age
00100	Slater	Christian	21
00200	Lannister	Kerry	20
00300	Hall	Lenny	22
00400	Daniels	Willy	20
00500	Hanson	Gilbert	23

Examples for ALIAS for tables:

The table EnrolledStudents will be represented with the small letter e, while the StudentsCourse will be represented with the small letter s.

Example: SELECT e.Last, e.First, s.course

FROM   EnrolledStudents AS e, StudentsCourse AS s

WHERE s.course = BSMT
AND e.IDNo = s.IDNo;

The resulting table will appear this way:

Last	First	Course
Slater	Christian	BSMT
Daniels	Willy	BSMT

You may add more conditions, depending on the table you would want to view or retrieve.

Chapter 33: Using the IN Operator

The IN operator is commonly used with the WHERE clause in a SQL query in specifying values.

The basic SQL syntax for the IN operator appears below.

Example: SELECT   "column_name1", "column_name2, ...

FROM "table_name'

WHERE   "column_name' IN (value1, value2, value3, ...);

Sample table

OnlineStudents

Name	Age	Average	City	Country
Paterson, Diana	25	85	Chicago	USA

Cruz, Tom	21	91	Madrid	Spain
Walters, Ken	25	84	Vancouver	Canada
Leonard, Alex	23	87	New York	USA
White, John	20	78	Los Angeles	USA

Example: SELECT *

FROM OnlineStudents

WHERE Country IN ('USA', 'Spain');

This SQL statement will produce a table that appears this way:

Name	Age	Average	City	Country
Paterson,	25	85	Chicago	USA

Diana				
Cruz, Tom	21	91	Madrid	Spain
Leonard, Alex	23	87	New York	USA
White, John	20	78	Los Angeles	USA

As a beginner learning SQL, this is a significant operator for you because you will be using it often in creating basic SQLs.

Chapter 34: Using CLONE TABLES

CLONE TABLES are identical tables that you can create to perform particular SQL tasks.

These CLONE TABLES have exactly the same format and content with the original table, so you won't have problems practicing on them first.

Tables that are retrieved by using CREATE TABLE SELECT may not have the same indexes and other values as the original, so CLONE TABLES are best in this aspect.

You can do this by using the MySQL with the following steps:

1. **Retrieve the complete structure of your selected table.**

   Obtain a CREATE TABLE query by displaying the CREATE TABLE keywords.

2. **Rename the table and create another one.**

   Change the "table_name" to your CLONE TABLE name. After, you submit the query, you will have two identical tables.

3. Execute step #2 and your CLONE TABLE is created.

4. To retain the data in the table, use the keyword INSERT INTO and SELECT.

Purposes of CLONE TABLES

- To create sample tables that you can work on without being fearful you would destroy the whole table.

- To act as practice tables for beginners, so that the tables in the databases are safe and protected.

- To feature new interface for new users.

- To protect the integrity of the tables in your databases from new users.

CLONE TABLES can be very useful, if utilized properly. Use them to your advantage.

Chapter 35: Using SQL EXPRESSIONS

SQL EXPRESSIONS make use of operators, characters, values and SQL functions that are combined to form a formula.

Numeric expressions

This expression is essential when forming SQL statements, where mathematical operations are needed.

The basic statement for this is:

Example: SELECT   expression   AS operational_name

FROM "table_name"

WHERE condition;

Boolean Expressions

These are expressions that are used in matching single values.

The basic statement for this is:

Example: SELECT   "column_name1", "column_name2"

FROM "table_name"

WHERE SINGLE VALUE MATCHING EXPRESSION;

Sample table

Sales

Name	TotalSales	ItemsSold	Date
Paterson, Diana	100.00	10	2/20/2016
Cruz, Tom	350.00	35	1/10/2016
Leonard, Alex	230.00	23	3/4/2016
White, John	420.00	42	4/26/2016
Brown, Dave	390.00	39	5/4/2016

If you want to extract the date of the TotalSales that is equivalent to 100, you can use this SQL statement:

Example: SELECT *

FROM Sales

WHERE TotalSales = 100;

Your resulting table would look like this:

Sales

Name	TotalSales	ItemsSold	Date
Paterson, Diana	100.00	10	2/20/2016

Date expressions

Date expressions are used for dates, understandably. They help extract the time values, and sometimes the current system date.

The basic SQL may appear like this:

Example: SELECT GETDATE ();

These are the SQL expressions that you can use according to the data you want to retrieve.

Chapter 36: Using VIEWS in SQL

VIEWS are virtual tables or stored SQL queries in the databases that have predefined queries and unique names. They are actually the resulting tables from your SQL queries.

As a beginner, you may want to learn about how you can use VIEWS. Among their numerous uses is their flexibility can combine rows and columns from VIEWS.

Here are important pointers and advantages in using VIEWS:

1. You can summarize data from different tables, or a subset of columns from various tables.

2. You can control what users of your databases can see, and restrict what you don't want them to view.

3. You can organize your database for your users' easy manipulation, while simultaneously protecting your non-public files.

4. You can modify, or edit, or UPDATE your data. Sometimes there are limitations, though, such

as, being able to access only one column when using VIEW.

5. You can create columns from various tables for your reports.

6. You should increase the security of your databases because VIEWS can display only the information that you want displayed. You can protect specific information from other users.

7. You can provide easy and efficient accessibility or access paths to your data to users.

8. You can allow users of your databases to derive various tables from your data without dealing with the complexity of your databases.

9. You can rename columns through views. If you are a website owner, VIEWS can also provide domain support.

10. The WHERE clause in the SQL VIEWS query may not contain subqueries.

11. For the INSERT keyword to function, you must include all NOT NULL columns from the original table.

12. Do not use the WITH ENCRIPTION (unless utterly necessary) clause for your VIEWS because you may not be able to retrieve the SQL.

13. Avoid creating VIEWS for each base table (original table). This can add more workload in managing your databases. As long as you create your base SQL query properly, there is no need to create VIEWS for each base table.

14. VIEWS that use the DISTINCT and ORDER BY clauses or keywords may not produce the expected results.

15. VIEWS can be updated under the condition that the SELECT clause may not contain the summary functions; and/or the set operators, and the set functions.

16. When UPDATING, there should be a synchronization of your base table with your VIEWS table. Therefore, you must analyze the VIEW table, so that the data presented are still correct, each time you UPDATE the base table.

17. Avoid creating VIEWS that are unnecessary because this will clutter your catalogue.

18. Specify "column_names" clearly.

19. The FROM clause of the SQL VIEWS query may not contain many tables, unless specified.

20. The SQL VIEWS query may not contain HAVING or GROUP BY.

21. The SELECT keyword can join your VIEW table with your base table.

How to create VIEWS

You can create VIEWS through the following easy steps:

Step #1 - Check if your system is appropriate to implement VIEW queries.

Step #2 - Make use of the CREATE VIEW SQL statement.

Step #3 – Use key words for your SQL syntax just like with any other SQL main queries.

Step #4 – Your basic CREATE VIEW statement or syntax will appear like this:

Example: Create view view_"table_name AS

SELECT "column_name1"

FROM "table_name"

WHERE [condition];

Let's have a specific example based on our original table.

EmployeesSalary

Names	Age	Salary	City
Williams, Michael	22	30000.00	Casper
Colton, Jean	24	37000.00	San Diego
Anderson, Ted	30	45000.00	Laramie
Dixon, Allan	27	43000.00	Chicago
Clarkson, Tim	25	35000.00	New York

Alaina, Ann	32	41000.00	Ottawa
Rogers, David	29	50000.00	San Francisco
Lambert, Jancy	38	47000.00	Los Angeles
Kennedy, Tom	27	34000.00	Denver
Schultz, Diana	40	46000.00	New York

Based on the table above, you may want to create a view of the customers' name and the City only. This is how you should write your statement.

Example: CREATE VIEW EmployeesSalary_VIEW AS

SELECT Names, City

FROM EmployeesSalary;

From the resulting VIEW table, you can now create a query such as the statement below.

SELECT * FROM EmployeesSalary_VIEW;

This SQL query will display a table that will appear this way:

EmployeesSalary

Names	City
Williams, Michael	Casper
Colton, Jean	San Diego
Anderson, Ted	Laramie
Dixon, Allan	Chicago
Clarkson, Tim	New York
Alaina, Ann	Ottawa
Rogers, David	San Francisco
Lambert, Jancy	Los Angeles
Kennedy, Tom	Denver
Schultz, Diana	New York

Using the keyword WITH CHECK OPTION

These keywords ascertain that there will be no return errors with the INSERT and UPDATE returns, and that all conditions are fulfilled properly.

Example: CREATE VIEW "table_Name"_VIEW AS

SELECT "column_name1", "column_name2"

FROM "table_name"

WHERE [condition]

WITH CHECK OPTION;

Applying this SQL statement to the same conditions (display name and city), we can come up now with our WITH CHECK OPTION statement.

Example: CREATE VIEW EmployeesSalary_VIEW AS

SELECT Names, City

FROM EmployeesSalary

WHERE City IS NOT NULL

WITH CHECK OPTION;

The SQL query above will ensure that there will be no NULL returns in your resulting table.

DROPPING VIEWS

You can drop your VIEWS whenever you don't need them anymore. The SQL syntax is the same as the main SQL statements.

Example: DROP VIEW EmployeesSalary_VIEW;

UPDATING VIEWS

You can easily UPDATE VIEWS by following the SQL query for main queries.

Example: CREATE OR REPLACE VIEW "tablename"_VIEWS (could also be VIEWS_'tablename") AS

SELECT "column_name"

FROM "table_name"

WHERE condition;

DELETING VIEWS

The SQL syntax for DELETING VIEWS is much the same way as DELETING DATA using the main SQL query. The difference only is in the name of the table.

If you use the VIEW table example above, and want to delete the City column, you can come up with this SQL statement.

Example: DELETE FROM EmployeesSalary_VIEW

WHERE City = 'New York';

The SQL statement above would have this output:

EmployeesSalary

Names	Age	Salary	City
Williams, Michael	22	30000.00	Casper
Colton, Jean	24	37000.00	San Diego
Anderson, Ted	30	45000.00	Laramie
Dixon, Allan	27	43000.00	Chicago
Alaina, Ann	32	41000.00	Ottawa
Rogers, David	29	50000.00	San

			Francisco
Lambert, Jancy	38	47000.00	Los Angeles
Kennedy, Tom	27	34000.00	Denver

INSERTING ROWS

Creating an SQL in INSERTING ROWS is similar to the UPDATING VIEWS syntax. Make sure you have included the NOT NULL columns.

Example: INSERT INTO "table_name"_VIEWS "column_name1"

WHERE value1;

VIEWS can be utterly useful, if you utilize them appropriately.

Chapter 37: SQL and Subqueries

In SQL, subqueries are queries within queries. The subqueries usually use the WHERE clause. Also called nested query or internal query, subqueries can also restrict the data being retrieved.

Creating subqueries are more complex than creating simple queries. You have to use essential key words such as, SELECT, DELETE, UPDATE, INSERT and the operators such as, BETWEEN (used only WITHIN a subquery and not WITH a subquery), IN, =, < =, > =, >, <, < >, and similar symbols.

In the previous chapters we have used subqueries a lot of times with the key word WHERE.

In this chapter, we would learn more about this vital keyword that is considered by many database programmers as the heart of SQL.

In composing a subquery, you have to remember these pointers.

1. It must be enclosed with an open and close parentheses.

2. It can be used in several ways.

3. It is recommended that a subquery can run on its own.

4. It can ascribe column values for files.

5. It can be found anywhere in the main query. You can identify it because it is enclosed in parentheses.

6. If it displays more than one row in response to an SQL command, this can only be accepted when there are multiple value operators. Example is the IN operator.

7. In a subquery, the GROUP BY is used instead of the ORDER BY, which is used in the main statement or query.

8. When creating subqueries, do not enclose it immediately in a set function.

9. To create subqueries, it is easier to start with a FROM statement.

10. Subqueries should also have names for easy identification.

11. When using the SELECT key word, only one column should be included in your subquery. The exception is when the main query has selected many columns for comparison.

12. Values that refer to a National Character Large Object (NCLOB), Binary Large Object (BLOB), Character Large Object (CLOB) and an Array, which is part of a collection data in variable

sizes, should NOT be included in your SELECT list.

There are several examples already from the previous chapters, but here are more:

Example #1 – Subqueries with SELECT key word or statement

SELECT   "column_name1"   FROM "table_name1"

WHERE value IN (SELECT "column_name2" FROM "table_name2' WHERE condition);

The above SQL query and subquery could also be written this way:

SELECT "column_name1"

FROM "table_name1"

WHERE value IN

(SELECT "column_name2"

FROM "table_name2 WHERE condition);

Let's apply the SQL statement in the two tables below:

Address

Street	City	State
67 7th St.	Los Angeles	California
10 18th St.	Casper	Wyoming
1020 Quincy Ave.	Chicago	Illinois
1019 Reed Ave.	Cheyenne	Wyoming
23 18th St.	San Diego	California

Online_Employees

Name	State	Age
Sarah Hawkins	Colorado	56
Noel Stevens	Florida	55
Lena Dawson	Minnesota	26
Timothy Pearson	Alaska	29
Allen Bailey	Wyoming	43

Your SQL query or statement would appear like this:

Example: SELECT State

FROM Address

WHERE City IN

(SELECT State

FROM Online_Employees

WHERE Age = > 60);

The above SQL query can be expressed without indentation, but programmers prefer to indent because this identifies more easily the subqueries or inner and outer queries.

SELECT State FROM Address WHERE City IN

(SELECT Age FROM Online_Employees

WHERE Age = > 60);

Use your subqueries properly to extract the data you need. You can review the subqueries that were discussed in the previous chapters.

Chapter 38: How SQL Injections Can Destroy Databases

Your databases can be destroyed easily by malicious persons with SQL injections. These thoughtless hackers can insert a code into your SQL statements through the web and damage your databases.

Hence, if you have plans of creating your own website, you must be aware of this so that you can avoid or prevent it from happening. The most common method is to hack into passwords and user names or IDs.

Hackers usually insert a number or a symbol that can change the returns of your SQL query.

Here's how you can minimize this incident from happening.

1. Create a BLACKLIST of words that are not allowed in the SQL statements submitted. If you are a website administrator, you will be screening out and minimizing the hacking of your website.

   This is not a full proof protection though, because most of the characters and symbols in SQL statements or queries are commonly used.

2. Utilize SQL PARAMETERS after your SQL query has been submitted. The symbol of PARAMETERS is @ .

Example #1: SELECT * FROM Visitors WHERE VisitorId = @0";

Example #2: INSERT INTO Students (StudentName, Age, City) Values (@1, @2, @3);

In the examples above, a malicious code (number) could not be inserted because the parameters have limited any addition of a new number.

3. Double check your SQL queries or syntax, so that this cannot be easily tampered with.

4. If you are a database user, submit your queries to websites that are proven legitimate.

5. If you are unsure of your SQL syntax, don't input it or be nonchalant about it. When uncertain, don't use it.

Although, not all SQL users will be concerned with hacking, it pays to know these basic prevention skills and be on the lookout for these malicious codes.

Chapter 39: Additional Pointers in Using SQL

There are significant pointers that you must know as a SQL beginner. Take note of them and enrich your SQL learning process.

1. **Be aware that there may be other versions of the SQL queries**. SQL has been extraordinarily helpful in modifying tables that many developers had created SQL syntax for their own applications. So, be open to new SQL statements.

2. **Ensure that your computer is durable, if you plan to establish your own database**. A computer that is not protected from viruses may have all of its databases corrupted.

3. **Be patient in learning.** There are no shortcuts to success; you have to go through the ups and downs.

4. **Persistence is the key**. No matter how hard the task is, if you are persistent and you persevere, you will never fail. As the cliche goes: A quitter never wins, and a winner NEVER quits."

5. **Be positive.** An optimistic attitude will help you learn more quickly. This is because you are

motivated in searching for the positive things that await you.

6. **Learn one chapter at a time.** No one is keeping tab of the time, so take your time. Munch the information slowly until your mind has digested the information sufficiently.

7. **Learn the limitations of your DBMS (database management system).** It is only in knowing this that you can modify your tables effectively.

8. **Avoid taxing your SQL server by creating unnecessary queries.** If you don't need all the columns, refrain from using * and select only the columns that you need. Submitting useless queries will only slow down your system.

9. **There are certain SQL statements that can be easier to use in fetching tables**. Remember the queries and apply whichever is more preferable for you.

10. **Ascertain that your 'table_names" are unique and have a fully qualified name**. You would not want retrieving two tables when all you needed is one. It is time consuming. Time is gold.

11. **Practice makes perfect;** therefore, do not be afraid to practice on some SQL databases or tables.

12. **Invite a friend to learn SQL with you.** Many beginners prefer to learn with someone. This is due to the fact that they can challenge

and motivate each other. But, of course, if you prefer learning alone, then that would not be a problem.

13. **Keep a logbook of your learning activities**. Through this method, you can monitor your progress and assess your knowledge.

14. **Apply what you have learned.** Learning can only be verified when you are able to apply it, so don't be afraid to create and tweak your own databases.

15. **Share your knowledge with others**. As you share it, you are also mastering and retaining the information more effectively.

These are simple tips that can help you optimize your SQL learning process. Apply them and be a master SQL expert eventually.

Chapter 40: SQL Quiz

Okay, so are you ready now to test how much you have learned about basic SQL?

10 questions to test your basic knowledge about SQL syntax or queries.

All SQL statements should be based on this table:

EmployeesSalary

Names	Age	Salary	City
Williams Michael	22	30000.00	Casper
Colton Jean	24	37000.00	San Diego
Anderson Ted	30	45000.00	Laramie
Dixon Allan	27	43000.00	Chicago
Clarkson Tim	25	35000.00	New York
Alaina Ann	32	41000.00	Ottawa
Rogers David	29	50000.00	San Francisco
Lambert Jancy	38	47000.00	Los Angeles

| Kennedy Tom | 27 | 34000.00 | Denver |
| Schultz Diana | 40 | 46000.00 | New York |

Answer the questions first before looking at the correct answers. Here goes:

1. Transcribe SQL.

2. What is the keyword in creating tables?

3. What is the SQL syntax in selecting tables?

4. What is the keyword in deleting tables?

5. What is the SQL statement if you want to display only the names and the city of the table above?

6. What is the SQL statement if you want to retrieve only the data of employees who are 25 years old and above?

7. What is the SQL command if you want to arrange the names in an ascending order?

8. What is the SQL query if you want to fetch the data of employees, who have a salary of more than 20000.00?

9. What is the SQL command if you want to select only the employees coming from Denver?

10. What is the SQL if you want to change the Name of Lambert Jancy to Walker Jean?

Easy? Oh yes! You should know the answers, as a beginner.

Try to answer all of them first, before checking on the correct answers.

Now, let's check if you have the correct answers.

ANSWERS:

1. STRUCTURED QUERY LANGUAGE

2. CREATE TABLE

3. SELECT "column_name1", "column_name2" FROM "table_name";

   (Remember to remove the double quotes when substituting the names of your columns and tables.)

4. DELETE TABLE

5. SELECT Names, City FROM EmployeesSalary;

6. SELECT * FROM EmployeesSalary
   WHERE Age >= 25;

7. SELECT * FROM EmployeesSalary
   ORDER BY Names ASC;

8. SELECT * FROM EmployeesSalary
   WHERE Salary >20000;

9. SELECT * FROM EmployeesSalary
   WHERE City = 'Denver';

10. UPDATE EmployeesSalary
    SET Names = 'Walker Jean'
    WHERE Names = 'Lambert Jancy';

How many correct answers did you get?

They are easy questions. I hope you got a perfect score. If not, then no sweat! Just review the chapters again and repeat the quiz.

Take note that the keywords such as, UPDATE, goes hand in hand with SET and WHERE.

UPDATE, SET WHERE. This is only one item, so create your own 'MEMORY NOTES'.

Conclusion

Learning the SQL language can be laborious and tedious, but if you have genuine interest in learning a new language and updating your skills, it could be relatively easy.

In this book, all the basic information that you need to learn as a beginner are presented. All you have to do is to apply them.

Now that you have read the book, you can go back for the details that you may forget along the way.

If you have properly studied the contents of this book, you could construct your basic SQL syntax easily.

Python Programming

A Beginner's Guide

Preface

The presentation of the contents in this book is done in an easy-to-understand language. This would help you comprehend better. In addition, the simple instructions will ensure that the procedures are understood first, before they are executed, or run.

I hope you enjoy it!

Contents

Chapter 1: Introduction to Python

In this generation of computer programming and highly technical applications, it's smart to move with the times. If you don't, you will be left behind in many undertakings that you want to pursue.

If you want to be the cream of the crop, you must learn how to create and read computer or programming language. Your knowledge will not only set you apart from your contemporaries, but will also boost your productivity and self-advancement in relevance with the expanding world of computer lingo.

What is Python?

Python is a powerful programming language. You can use it for free in developing software that can run on Nokia mobile phones, Windows, Mac OS X, Linux, Unix, JAVA, Amiga, and many more operating systems.

Python is object-oriented and provides simple and easy to read and use language that you can utilize in creating your programs.

Even if you're not a programmer, it would be beneficial for you to know about Python because of the numerous uses you can take advantage of.

So, where is Python used?

Here is a summary of the uses of Python:

1. To process images
2. To write Internet scripts
3. To embed scripts
4. To manipulate database programs
5. To provide system utilities
6. To create artificial intelligence
7. To create graphical user interface applications using IDEs on Windows and other platforms

Advantages of learning Python

For you to understand more what you stand to gain from learning Python, here are its major pros.

You can:

1. Learn Python easily because the syntax or language in programming is simple.
2. Prepare codes readily that can be used in various operating systems such as Linux, Windows, Unix and Mac OS X.
3. Promptly access the Python standard library that helps users in creating, editing, accessing, running and maintaining files.
4. Integrate programs and systems promptly because the programming language is easy to follow.
5. Handle the errors more reliably because the syntax is capable of identifying and raising exceptions.
6. Learn more quickly because the programming language is object-oriented.

7. Access IDLE, which makes it possible for users to create codes and check if the codes work, through Python's interactive system.
8. Download Python for free, and enjoy all the benefits of a free application.
9. Embed your Python data in other systems.
10. Stop worrying about freeing the memory for your codes, because Python does it automatically.

If you're in, then, let's start the ball rolling!

Chapter 2: How to Install Python

In this time and age, being techy is a demand of the times, and the lack of knowledge, classifies one as an outback. This can result to being left out from the career world, especially in the field of programming.

Numerous big shot companies have employed their own programs for purposes of branding, and to cut back on IT expenses.

In the world of programming, using Python language is found to be easier and programmer-friendly, thus, the universal use.

Discussed below are information on how to download python for MS Windows. In this particular demo, we have chosen windows because it's the most common worldwide – even in not so progressive countries. We want to cater to the programming needs of everyone all over the globe.

Python 2.7.12 version was selected because this version bridges the gap between the old version 2 and the new version 3.

Some of the updated functions/applications of version 3 are still not compatible with some devices, so 2.7.12 is a smart choice.

Steps in downloading Python 2.7.12, and installing it on Windows

1. *Type python on your browser and press the Search button to display the search results.*

Scroll down to find the item you are interested in. In this instance, you are looking for python. click "python releases for windows", and a new page opens. See image below:

2. *Select the Python version, Python 2.7.12, and click, or you can select the version that is compatible to your device or OS.*

Python Releases for Windows

- Latest Python 2 Release - Python 2.7.12

- Latest Python 3 Release - Python 3.5.2

- Python 3.6.0b1 - 2016-09-12
    - Download Windows x86 web-based installer
    - Download Windows x86 executable installer
    - Download Windows x86 embeddable zip file
    - Download Windows x86-64 web-based installer
    - Download Windows x86-64 executable installer
    - Download Windows x86-64 embeddable zip file
    - Download Windows help file
- Python 3.6.0a4 - 2016-08-15
    - Download Windows x86 web-based installer
    - Download Windows x86 executable installer
    - Download Windows x86 embeddable zip file
    - Download Windows x86-64 web-based installer
    - Download Windows x86-64 executable installer
    - Download Windows x86-64 embeddable zip file

3. *The new page contains the various python types. Scroll down and select an option: in this instance, select Windows x86 MSI installer and click.*

Files

Version	Operating System	Description	MD5 Sum	File Size	GPG
Gzipped source tarball	Source release		88d61f82e3616a4be962828b3694109d	16935940	SIG
XZ compressed source tarball	Source release		57dffcee9cee8bb2ab5f82af1d6e9a60	12390820	SIG
Mac OS X 32-bit i386/PPC installer	Mac OS X	for Mac OS X 10.5 and later	3adbedcc935a0db1ab08aa41f3ec4e33	24214626	SIG
Mac OS X 64-bit/32-bit installer	Mac OS X	for Mac OS X 10.6 and later	86bcddc2bccd27335d27aa0d7e4952c1	22265024	SIG
Windows debug information files	Windows		1751598e16431be04e1f4f24ca52b53a	24678566	SIG
Windows debug information files for 64-bit binaries	Windows		c5433a7fca9ede6e52835bd40e40aa8d	25481382	SIG
Windows help file	Windows		7bc4e15ecae8ede7c8fe122f0a6d5f27	6224175	SIG
Windows x86-64 MSI installer	Windows	for AMD64/EM64T/x64, not Itanium processors	8fa13925dba7638aa472a3e794ca4ee3	19820644	SIG
Windows x86 MSI installer	Windows		fe0ef5b8fd02722f32f7284324934f9d	18907136	SIG

4. *Press the Python box at the bottom of your screen.*

Click the "Run" button, and wait for the new window to appear.

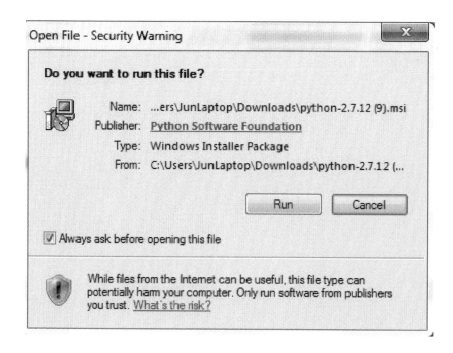

Open File - Security Warning

Do you want to run this file?

Name: ...ers\JunLaptop\Downloads\python-2.7.12 (9).msi
Publisher: Python Software Foundation
Type: Windows Installer Package
From: C:\Users\JunLaptop\Downloads\python-2.7.12 (...

Run   Cancel

☑ Always ask before opening this file

While files from the Internet can be useful, this file type can potentially harm your computer. Only run software from publishers you trust. What's the risk?

5. *Select the user options that you require and press "NEXT".*

Your screen will display the hard drive where your python will be located.

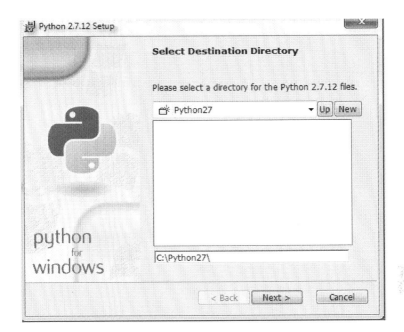

6. Press the "NEXT" button.

7. Press yes, and wait for a few minutes. Sometimes it can take longer for the application to download, depending on the speed of your internet.

8. After that, click the FINISHED button to signify that the installation has been completed

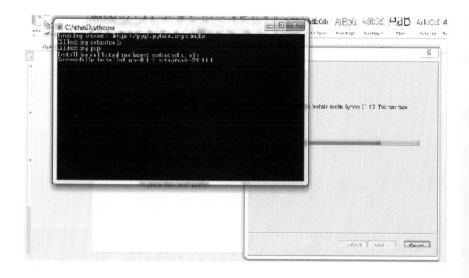

Your python has been installed in your computer and is now ready to use. Find it in drive C, or wherever you have saved it.

There can be errors along the way, but there are options which are presented in this book. If you follow it well, there is no reason that you cannot perform this task.

It's important to note that there's no need to compile programs. Python is an interpretive language and can execute quickly your commands.

You can also download directly from the Python website, by selecting any of these versions – 3.5.2 or 2.7.12. and clicking 'download'. (For this book, 2.7.12 is used, in general, for easy discussions).

See image below*:*

Follow the step by step instructions prompted by the program itself. Save and run the program in your computer.

For Mac

To download Python on Mac, you can follow a similar procedure, but this time, you will have to access the "Python.mpkg" file, to run the installer.

For Linux

For Linux, Python 2 and 3 may have been installed by default. Hence, check first your operating system. You can check if your device has already a Python program, by accessing your command prompt and entering this: python—version, or python3—version.

If Python is not installed in Linux, the result "command not found" will be displayed. You may want to download both Python 2.7.12 and any of the versions of Python 3 for your Linux. This is because Linux can have more compatibility with Python 3.

For Windows users, now that you have downloaded the program, you're ready to start.

And yes, congratulations! You can now begin working and having fun with your Python programming system.

Chapter 3: Basic Python Terms You Must Learn

As previously described, Python is a language used in computer programming. As such, you must be familiar with the most commonly used lingo to facilitate your understanding of the language. It's like learning the ABCs before you can read or write your first letters.

Remember that there may be slight variations with the different Python versions. The example here is from version 2. So, here goes:

1. **Strings** – are the values enclosed inside double, single quotes, or triple quotes. They can be a word/text, or a group of words, or a Unicode, or other items.

   Example:

   mystring = 'welcome'

   mystring = "welcome"

   mystring = 'My little corner.'

   mystring = "My little corner."

   - The advantage of the double quotes is that you can include values within the double quotes.

   - The triple quotes signify long or lengthy strings. They are useful to avoid getting an EOL (End of the Line) error.

2. **Variables** – are containers for the strings. In the Python language, these are usually objects. These can be numbers or strings. Remember that you have to declare the variables, prior to using them.

    The numbers can be floating point numbers or integers.

    Use this syntax to define integers and floating point numbers. Integers are whole numbers, while floating point numbers are usually numbers with decimal points.

    Example:

    myint = 9

    myfloat = 9.0

    A more detailed explanation is presented in chapters 4 & 7.

3. **Statements** – are stated sentences or syntax used to call a function to compute, to write a value, or other procedures needed in executing or performing Python commands. There are several types of statements, which will be discussed in chapter 6 and other chapters of this book.

4. **Lists** – are just like your ordinary lists for items you want to create. They can contain any variable/s that you want to include in your list. They can be comparable to arrays. The variables are usually enclosed in brackets, and the items or values are

separated by commas. The semi-colon can be used between lists. Lists are immutable files – meaning they cannot be changed. More about this on the succeeding chapters.

The word-values are enclosed in single or double quotes, while numbers are not.

Example:

mylist1 = ['chemistry', 'anatomy', 2015, 2016];

mylist2 = [10, 20, 30, 40, 50];

mylist3 = ['grades', 'names', 'addresses]

When you add the function 'print' and press 'enter' or execute, this will appear:

Take note of the variations of colors that can identify the command or function (red colored word), from the variables (green), and from the results (blue colored words).

Examples of double quotes:

mystring4=["Vanessa Redgrave", "Tom Cruise", "Mel Gibson", "Matt Damon"]

5. **Loops** – are statements that can be performed or executed one after the other – repeatedly, or once. There are two general types of loops, the 'for' and the 'while' loops. Read more about loops in chapter 25.

6. **Function** – a piece of chord that executes some functions or logic. Examples are 'print', which prints your entry or variables; pow (power), which gets the answer for your numbers raised to a certain power. A specific example is this:

To know the value of 8^9, you can use the Python function (pow). On your Python shell enter this statement:

pow(8,9)

When you press the 'enter' or the execute key, the answer will appear:

In the specific example above, the answer is 134217728.

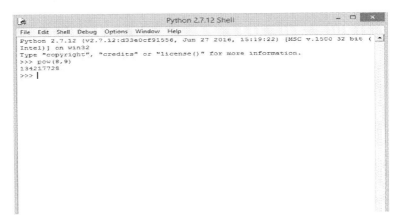

There are still various Python functions that will be discussed in the next chapters.

7. **Modules** – are files that contain various items, such as variables, definitions of functions, and executable statements, among others. Modules are used in cases when you want to save functions that you have created for easier accessibility later on.

This is because after using the Python interpreter, all the definitions, variables and functions you have created will be lost. Hence, you need to compile them in modules, so you can use them again, whenever necessary.

Python will automatically ask you to save your files, so you will never forget this function. Your modules should be saved with the name you assigned to them, and the suffix - .py.

It's best to assign names based on the object, or the purpose of your module. This way, you can recall the names of the modules easily.

8. **Shells** – are the blank boxes where you write your Python commands or statements.

9. **Tuples** – are similar to lists; they are immutable. You cannot change them. However, you can create new Tuples to modify the old ones. They can also be used as keys to dictionaries. Tuples will be discussed more in chapter 26.

10. **Classes** – are groups of related data, similar to strings, integers, and lists that use related functions. To introduce or identify a class, you can use the function word 'class'.

11. **Objects** – are used in Python language a great deal, because Python is object-oriented. This means that the user can name his files according to what they are as a group, or as an individual value. An example is when a user names his data about Geography as 'Geo", or his research data on climate change, as 'climchange'.

12. **Concatenation** – a series of connected strings or variables use in Python programs. You can combine small strings to become larger strings by utilizing the 'join'( ) procedure or the plus (+) sign.

There will be more Python terms that you will encounter as we proceed. Not all of them is included here.

But don't worry, the new terms will be defined as we use them in the succeeding chapters.

Chapter 4: Functions of the Python Standard Library

The Python standard library is one of the most extensive libraries in the world of programming. This is because it contains all the possible packages and modules that a programmer would need.

There are various reference materials, modules, significant built-in functions, and packaging tools to assist you in learning the Python language.

The common functions of a standard library are:

- It provides built-in modules that are easily accessible for programmers, who may encounter problems in creating and executing their codes.

- It acts as a guide to experts, who want prompt and reliable methods of creating and running their programs.

- It allows quick access to Python's system functionality and enhances programmer's output.

- It can also provide optional components essential to programming that comes from third parties.

In the Python standard library, an introduction is provided and then the essential materials follow. Here are some of the most basic contents of a Python standard library together with their specific functions.

1. **Built-in Functions** (types, constants and exceptions) - these are components that come with the Python package. You can call in these functions when you need them, and when you need help in creating your statements.

These built-in functions are readily available to Python users:

Here are some of the most common functions:

- **abs( )** – this function is used when you want to determine the absolute value of a particular number.

```
>>>
>>> abs(35)
35
>>>
>>>
```

- **all( ), all(iterable)** - this function will return a 'True' result with a blank iterable, and if ALL the iterable (taken one after the other) are True. Refer to the chapter on loops for examples and actual use.

- **any( ), any(iterable)** – this will return a 'True' result, if ANY element of the iterable is true. A 'False' result is printed, when the iterable is left blank.

- **basestring( )** – this will determine if the object is a Unicode or a string.

- **cmp( )** – this is the key for comparing elements in a data. It is most useful in tuple.

- **dict( )** – this refers to the dictionary class.

- **dir([object])** – this refers to the directory. There are some examples in the chapters of this book.

Example:

If you want to access the built-in directory, use this statement:

dir(["__builtin__"])

press 'enter' or execute and the built-in directory will appear:

- **getattr( ), getattr(object, name[, default])** – this function is used in returning the value of the attributes of the specified object.

- **help( )** – this function is used in asking help from the Python's built-in functions and modules. It's interactive and can help you with a lot of things you would want to learn.

- **input( ), input([prompt]), raw_input( )** – the input data can help in accessing history features and similar data.

- **int( ), class int(x, base=10), class int(x=0)** - this function is used to return an integer. The types of the numeric may be a float, a complex number, a long number or an integer.

- **len(s)** – this will display the length of the items or elements of an object.

- **map( ) – (function, iterable,...)** – this function returns a list that provides a function applied to each iterable.

- **open( ), (object(name[,mode[,buffering])** – this keyword opens the data specified and returns the results.

Where:

name = name of the file to be opened

mode = this is a type of string that specifies how the file will be opened. The values are 'r'-reading, 'w'-writing, and 'a' for appending.

- **range(stop), range(start(,stop[step])** – this is a function that is commonly used in loops because of its arithmetic progressions. It returns a list of integers. The return defaults to (1), when the start argument is blank, and defaults to (0), when the step argument is omitted.

- **reload(module)** – this function will reload the module you want to access. The module should have been loaded previously and imported successfully, but be aware that there are some modules that may not reload, once they have been loaded previously. So, remember to save your modules.

- **round(number[,ndigits])** – this function rounds off numbers to the specified ndigits, after the decimal point.

- **vars([object])** – this returns the value of a __dict__attribute, and can function as the local dictionary.

Some of the other built-in functions are not mentioned in the above-mentioned list because they are used in the examples in some of the chapters.

The complex ones are also omitted to prevent information overload ('too much, too soon'). You might end up learning nothing because of the tremendous amount of data that can suffocate your brain, making it unable to assimilate anything.

It's better to learn some basic Python programming language. and be able to retain them than gobbling all the information at one time.

2. **String Services** – strings are crucial in Python programming, and a complete information about strings is provided in chapters 16 to 19 .

3. **Data Types** – there are various data types that you must become familiar with, if you want to learn Python. These data types are sometimes handled differently.

4. **File and Directory Access** – You cannot access your files or data unless you know how.

5. **Numeric and Mathematical Modules** – Numerical computations are a part of the Python language. You can perform a number of data manipulations with these modules.

6. **Python (Runtime Services, Language and Interpreters, Compiler Package)** – the Python library is not complete without these packages. These are the programs that make Python work.

Anyway, you can access the built-in functions anytime you want; thus, you don't have to memorize all of them.

Below is an image of some of these built-in data in Python programming.

Name	Date modified	Type	Size
encodings	10/1/2016 10:09 AM	File folder	
ensurepip	9/30/2016 11:34 PM	File folder	
hotshot	10/1/2016 6:35 PM	File folder	
idlelib	10/9/2016 3:30 PM	File folder	
importlib	10/1/2016 12:02 AM	File folder	
json	9/30/2016 11:34 PM	File folder	
lib2to3	10/1/2016 6:35 PM	File folder	
lib-tk	10/1/2016 10:03 AM	File folder	
logging	9/30/2016 11:34 PM	File folder	
msilib	10/1/2016 6:35 PM	File folder	
multiprocessing	10/1/2016 6:35 PM	File folder	
pydoc_data	10/1/2016 6:35 PM	File folder	
site-packages	10/3/2016 3:25 PM	File folder	
sqlite3	10/1/2016 6:35 PM	File folder	
test	10/1/2016 6:35 PM	File folder	
unittest	10/1/2016 12:02 AM	File folder	
wsgiref	10/1/2016 6:35 PM	File folder	
xml	9/30/2016 11:34 PM	File folder	
__future__	6/25/2016 11:46 PM	Python File	5 KB
__future__	9/30/2016 11:34 PM	Compiled Python ...	5 KB

Aside from these, there are more optional services and modules that a user can utilize.

The Python programming language is extensive. If we were to discuss them all, it would take months to learn everything. So, let's choose the most significant parts that you can learn - given the circumstances.

Chapter 5: Basic Elements of Python

Learning the ABCs of anything in this world, is a must. Knowing the essentials is winning half the battle before you get started. It's easier to proceed when you are equipped with the fundamentals of what you are working on.

In the same manner that before you embark on the other aspects of python let us level off the basic elements first. You need to learn and understand the basics of python as a foundation in advancing to the more complicated components. This fundamental information will greatly help you as you go on and make the learning experience easier and enjoyable.

Familiarize yourself with the Python Official Website *https://www.python.org/*. Knowing well the website of python would give you the leverage in acquiring more information and scaling up your knowledge about python. Also, you can get the needed links for your work

Learn from Python collections. Locate python collections such as records, books, papers, files, documentation and archives and learn from it. You can pick up a number of lessons from these, and expand your knowledge about Python. There are also tutorials, communities and forums at your disposal.

Possess the SEO Basics. Acquire some education on Search Engine Optimization so you can interact with experts in the field and improve your python level of knowledge. Here are the basic elements of Python.

Basic elements of Python

Language and the programs

This is the phase where the program language is presented to make the user understand the type of language employed and knowing how to use it.

Interpretations and modules drafting

Python can be used as an active translator or transcriber by interaction through the web. It can also be employed to formulate lessons. In interaction, though, there is one serious concern: that is, it is impossible to keep a copy of what transpired. On the other hand, using lessons allows you to keep a record of the work done. In the interactive translator, you are allowed to open only one display page, while in lessons, there are no limits.

Variables

Python uses information that are not constant, these are used to keep the data. When using these, be sure to put descriptions. These data could be names, age, addresses, gender and other similar material.

Outputs and Inputs

Any computer program requires interfacing between itself and the person using it. The user encodes and that is input, and the output is printing what has been encoded.

Mathematics

Numbers are the common language in computer programs including Python. Mathematical operations are used by Python as you will learn later on. Most of its language is represented by mathematical equations and symbols.

Loop

You need to understand the term loop in python. It is a symbol used to represent repeated word/s or sentence/s in python programming. Anything that is being repeatedly used can employ a loop.

Python categories

You should get acquainted with the types of python product categories for easy reference and understanding. Python categories are symbolized by A, B, C that signifies the shifts in language. Examples are 3.3.1 to 3.3.2. This means there are minor changes, but when it employs something like 2.xx to 3.xx it means there are major changes.

Cutting

This is a critical component of python which is used to copy the desired part of a data. It is a method of making programs simple by concentrating on items from a gamut of data. When you do that, you are actually removing components that are not relevant to the program.

Modules

Modules are files of descriptions and declarations of Python. It is a list of all the terminologies used by python with corresponding explanations of each. Python adopts a method of consolidating definitions into one folder called **module**. These modules can be introduced into different modules depending on the needs of the program or user.

This is created to allow users to have a better understanding and easy access to the standard library of Python. A programmer or even a beginner can make modules for his use.

Modules can be on: Indexing and searching, Audio and Music, Web development, Console and Database. Python provides an array of modules that you can use. You can also make your own.

Source codes

Generating Python source codes can be tedious, if you don't know how to derive your codes.

Program developers have now an application that converts your Python 2 codes to Python version 3 codes from AST.

You can create your own code as discussed in the chapters, and it's easy to append strings to a list to create a code, but it won't hurt you, if you know how to generate Python source codes. You can use the context managers for this.

These are the most basic elements in python, there are more but with the ones presented, one can already start using python and learn the others, as you go on in your programming.

Chapter 6: Types of Python Statements

There are several types of Python statements that you must know. These statements will help you in creating your Python syntax/codes.

Here are the most common statements:

1. **Simple statements (simple_stmt)**

    These are statements that are composed of a single logical line. They may occur singly, or in several statements in one line. If there are several simple statements, they can be separated by a semicolon.

    The most common simple statement is the 'print' statement. You have also the 'delete' (del),'import', 'return', 'pass', 'continue', 'assignment', 'raise', 'break', to name some.

Example:

print var1

This means that the values in variable 1 (var1) will be printed. Of course, var1 has to be defined first by assigning the values prior to executing the 'print' command. There will be examples in the next chapters.

2. Assignment statements (assignment_stmt), (target), (target_list)

These statements are used when names are assigned to values, and when you want to modify mutable (can be changed) objects. The syntax is similar to that of the expression statements.

3. Expression statements (expression_stmt)

These statements are generally used for computations and for evaluating an expression list. They are also useful in writing values. They usually return the (none) value, when used to call a procedure.

4. import statements (import_stmt)

These are used to import files, functions or modules. Python has packages (directories) containing modules (files). You can quickly import modules by using the key 'import'.

Example:

I want to import my names1 and strings1 files; these are the statements:

import names1

import strings1

See image below:

```
>>>
>>> import names1
('Potter Richard', 'Walker Henry', 'Fell Don', 'Dean James', 20, 34, 41, 32)
```

```
>>>
>>> import strings1
Remember.911
>>>
```

If Python cannot find the file, it will return the 'ImportError'. You cannot import your files if you have not saved them. Likewise, you cannot import a file or module that is not part of the Python program.

You can use importlib.import module( ), when you want to know more about the modules.

5. continue Statements (continue_stmt)

These statements indicate that the statement, usually a loop, continues with the next loop. It's used with the 'for' or 'while' loop.

Example:

for letter in 'Walker':

   if letter == 'W':

      continue

print 'Current Letter:', letter

When 'Run' and 'Run Module' are clicked. The result that will appear in a new shell will be the rest of the letters of "Walker".

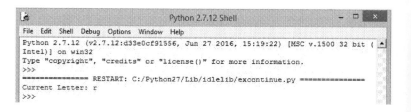

6. break statements (break_stmt)

These are statements that may occur in the 'for' or 'while' loops. Their function is to 'break' the nearest enclosing loop, and resumes execution on the next statement. But the loop will finally 'break' when the 'try' statement and the 'finally' clause are executed.

Example:

```
For letter in 'Walker':
  if letter == 'l':
    break
print 'Current Letter: ', letter
```

This 'break' statement will return these results:

Current Letter: W

Current Letter: a

This code will only return and print 'W' and 'a', which came before the break statement 'l'.

7. return Statements (return_stmt)

These statements are used usually in evaluating an expression list and exiting a function, operation or method. There are two forms the 'return' and 'return expressions'. They could be present in the definition of a function, but not in the definition of a nested class.

Example:


```
def doPrint():

    print "Clinical",

    return "Chemistry"

    print "is",

    return "interesting"
```

print doPrint()

See image below:

When 'Run' is clicked, the results printed are only 'Clinical Chemistry', because after the 'return' statement, the function will stop, so it won't print/display the rest of the entries after the 'return' statement.

See image below:

8. Else and Elif statements

These statements are discussed individually in chapters 23 and 24.

9. if Statements

These are statements that give an 'if' argument. It's often used with 'else' or 'elif' statements.

Example:

x= int(input("Please type a number: "))   # This is your base statement.

Please type a number:
        # This will appear, and you have

to type a number.

                                #
                                the'if'
                                conditi
                                on   is:

if x > 0:

    x=0

print 'You have a good number!'

You have a good number!   #If the number you typed is higher than zero(0), This will appear in the results.

The entire Python statement will be like this:

```python
x= int(input("Please type a number: "))
    if x > 0:
        x=0
    print 'You have a good number!'
```

See image below:

When you click 'Run', and then 'Run Module', the result will be a statement asking you to type a number:

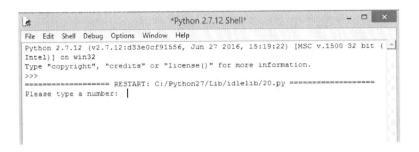

When you type 35, and press 'enter', this will be the result:

"You have a good number."

This is because this was the 'if' statement specified for values more than zero (0).

See image below:

There are still various statements used in Python, but for now, these are some of the essential types that are good to know.

Chapter 7: How to Start Using Python

Beginners may find it difficult to start using Python. It's a given and nothing's wrong about that. However, your desire to learn will make it easier for you to gradually become familiar with the language.

Here are the specific steps you can follow to start using Python.

Steps in using Python

Step #1 – Read all about Python.

Python has included a README information in your downloaded version. It's advisable to read it first, so you will learn more about the program.

You can start using your Python through the command box (black box), or you can go to your saved file and read first the README file by clicking it.

See image below:

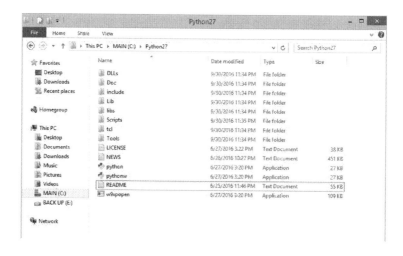

This box will appear.

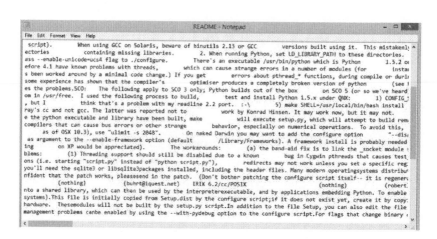

You can read the content completely, if you want to understand more what the program is all about, the file-setup, and similar information.

This is a long data that informs you of how to navigate and use Python. Also, Python welcomes new contributions for its further development.

You can copy paste the content of the box into a Window document for better presentation.

Step #2 – Start using Python.

First open the Python file you have saved in your computer. Click on Python as shown below. In some versions, you just click 'python' for the shell to appear.

See image below:

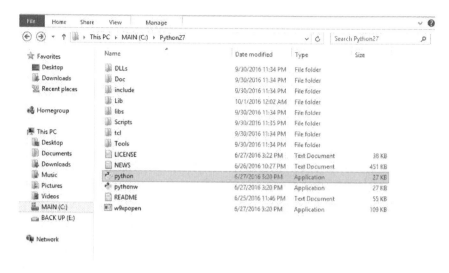

You can start using Python by utilizing the simplest function, which is 'print'. It's the simplest statement or directive of python. It prints a line or string that you specify.

For Python 2, print command may or may not be enclosed in parenthesis or brackets, while in Python 3 you have to enclose print with brackets.

Example for Python 2:

print "Welcome to My Corner."

Example for Python 3:

print ("Welcome to My Corner")

The image below appears when you press 'enter'.

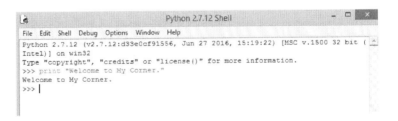

You may opt to use a Python shell through idle. If you do, this is how it would appear:

In the Python 3.5.2 version, the text colors are: function (purple), string (green) and the result (blue). (The string is composed of the words inside the bracket ("Welcome to My Corner"), while the function is the command word outside the bracket (print).

Take note that the image above is from the Python 2.7.12 version.

You have to use indentation for your Python statements/codes. The standard Python code uses four spaces. The indentations are used in place of braces or blocks.

In some programming languages, you usually use semi-colons at the end of the commands – in python, you don't need to add semi-colons at the end of the whole statement.

In Python, semi-colons are used in separating variables inside the brackets.

For version 3, click on your downloaded Python program and save the file in your computer. Then Click on IDLE (Integrated Development Environment), your shell will appear. You can now start using your Python. It's preferable to use idle, so that your codes can be interpreted directly by idle.

Alternative method to open a shell (for some versions).

An alternative method to use your Python is to open a shell through the following steps:

Step #1 – Open your menu.

After downloading and saving your Python program in your computer, open your menu and find your saved Python file. You may find it in the downloaded files of your computer or in the files where you saved it.

Step #2 – Access your Python file.

Open your saved Python file (Python 27) by double-clicking it. The contents of Python 27 will appear. Instead of clicking on Python directly (as shown above), click on Lib instead. See image below.

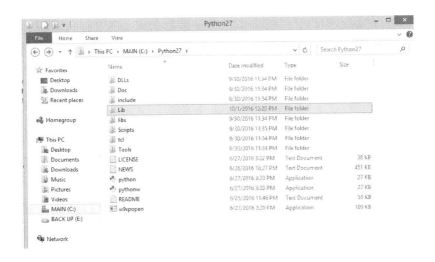

This will appear:

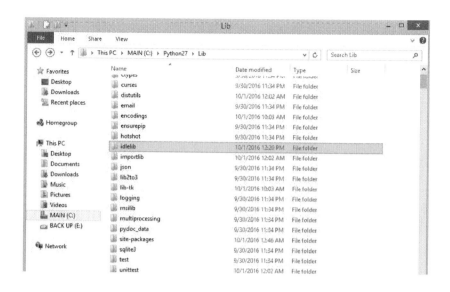

Step #3 – Click on 'idlelib'.

Clicking the 'idlelib' will show this content:

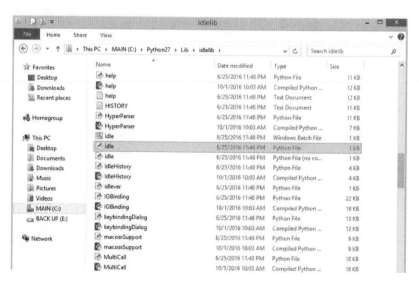

Step #4 – Click on idle to show the Python shell.

When you click on any of the 'idle' displayed on the menu, the 'white' shell will be displayed, as shown below:

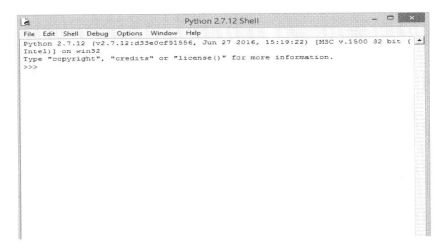

The differences between the three 'idle' menu, is that the first two 'idle' commands have the black box (shell) too, while the last 'idle' has only the 'white' box (shell). I prefer the third 'idle' because it's easy to use.

Step #5 – Start using your Python shell.

You can now start typing Python functions, using the shell above.

You may have noticed that there are various entries to the contents of each of the files that you have opened. You can click and open all of them, as you progress in learning more about your Python programming.

Python is a language that has been studied by students for several days or months. Thus, what's presented in this book are the basics for beginners.

Chapter 8: Basic Python Syntax Rules

Every language has its syntax rules. Python is no different. For Python, there are essential rules that you have to remember. Applying them will help you a lot in using Python correctly.

1. **Python statements are delimited, when you create a new line.**

   When you create a new line, or press enter on your keyboard, the old line will be discontinued or delimited - unless you use the reverse slash (\ ), the brackets (curly { } and square [ ]) and parentheses ( ), to indicate that the statement has not ended yet.

   Example:

   print ('hello')

   When you type this on your Python shell and press 'enter', it's the end of the statement.

```
Python 2.7.12 Shell                                      –  □  ×
File  Edit  Shell  Debug  Options  Window  Help
Python 2.7.12 (v2.7.12:d33e0cf91556, Jun 27 2016, 15:19:22) [MSC v.1500 32 bit (
Intel)] on win32
Type "copyright", "credits" or "license()" for more information.
>>> print('hello')
hello
>>>
```

2. **Python statements, or variables in brackets, can span several lines, without using the continuation symbol (\ ).** But ascertain that commas are written in between each item.

Variables or items enclosed with parentheses ( ), square brackets [ ], and curly brackets { } must be separated with commas, as well.

Example #1:

   x = [2,

   [4,

   [6,

   [8]

See image below:

```
*Python 2.7.12 Shell*
File  Edit  Shell  Debug  Options  Window  Help
Python 2.7.12 (v2.7.12:d33e0cf91556, Jun 27 2016, 15:19:22) [MSC v.1500 32 bit (
Intel)] on win32
Type "copyright", "credits" or "license()" for more information.
>>> print('hello')
hello
>>> x = [2,
        [4,
        [6,
        [8]
        |
```

Example #2:

Mystring=['alpha', 'beta', 'gamma']

See image below:

```
Python 2.7.12 Shell
File  Edit  Shell  Debug  Options  Window  Help
Python 2.7.12 (v2.7.12:d33e0cf91556, Jun 27 2016, 15:19:22) [MSC v.1500 32 bit (
Intel)] on win32
Type "copyright", "credits" or "license()" for more information.
>>>
>>>
>>> mystring=['alpha', 'beta', 'gamma']
>>>
>>>
```

3. **Variables can be placed in a single line, but they must be separated by semi-colons.**

Example:

print ('names', 'grades'); print (10, 20, 30); print ('addresses')

See image below:

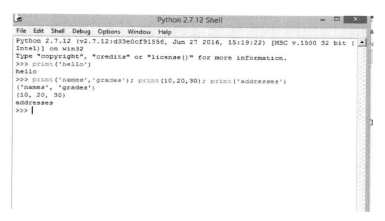

4. **When naming variables, use nouns in the lowercase.**

Examples:

names, patients, grades

If you want to use two words, to be more specific, you can use an underscore.

Examples:

names_patients

grades_students

Remember to enclose your variables using the single ('), or double quotes ("").

5. **When using functions, use a verb in the lowercase (small letters).**

Examples:

print, get, get area

When using two words, you can use an underscore to separate the two words.

Example:

get_area

6. **When using constant names, use a noun consisting of words using the uppercase, and separated by an underscore.**

Example:

MED_STUDENTS

7. **When using class names, the first letter of each word should be in the uppercase (capitalized).** This is called the camel-case.

Examples:

MyStudents

MyStrings

In some versions of Python, the first letter of the first word is expressed using the lowercase.

Examples:

myStudents

myString

Generally, Python is a case system program so take note of those items that make use of the lowercase (example: Python keywords), and those that make use of the uppercase as specified above.

8. **The Python body blocks should be properly indented** (generally 4 spaces – more or less - one-tab key in your keypad). This is a basic rule that you should apply when creating python syntax.

9. **When you want to continue to the next line, use the slash symbol (\).** This is to indicate that the next line is a continuation of the first.

Example:

```
ave=element1 + \
    element2 + \
    element3
```

10. **Always use quotes to enclose your string literals (word-strings).** Python recognizes single quotes (' '), double quotes (" "), and triple quotes (""" """) – for multiple lines. These quotes identify word-strings.

Examples:

string1=['anatomy',   'chemistry',   'physiology', 'histology']

string2= ["anatomy", "chemistry", "physiology", "histology"]

string3 =["""This is the flash story I wrote for the website. It's made up of 300 words."""]

See image below:

```
                          *Untitled*                    _  □  ×
File  Edit  Format  Run  Options  Window  Help
string1=['anatomy', 'chemistry', 'physiology', 'histology']

string2= ["anatomy", "chemistry", "physiology", "histology"]

string3 =["""This is the flash story I wrote for the website. It's made up of 30

|
```

11. **When creating multiple statements in a single line, remember to use a semi-colon (;).**

    Example:

    personnel = "Porky the Pig"; "Reed Avenue"; "College of Sciences";

    "Cheyenne Wyoming"

12. **When delimiting program blocks, use whitespaces or indentations.**

    Example:

    class EmployeeInfo:

      def __init__ (self) :

        print ("Employee Information Data.")

      def personalInfo(self, firstName, lastName) :

```
    self.firstName=firstName

    self.lastName=lastName

def printPersonalInfo(self) :

    print(self.firstName, ' ', self.lastName, ' ')
```

Observe the indentations of the sample statement above. If you change the indentation, the result will give an error.

The Python code/statement above will be discussed in chapter 14 on the topic about "Class".

These are some of the basic rules in Python syntax. The other rules will be discussed as we go on with the other chapters.

Chapter 9: Application of Python in Math and Numbers

There are various types of numbers supported by Python; these are complex, integers (int), long integers, and floating point real values. Simple codes/statements are introduced to give you the basics.

Beginners may find it daunting to use Python in solving simple mathematical and number problems. People fear what they don't know. The truth, however, is that with a little addition of codes or signs, it's as easy as using your ordinary calculator. Here's how to do it.

Step #1 – Open your Python command box.

Open your saved Python file through your start menu. Click on 'python' for version 2, and the IDLE GUI to open your 'shell' for version 3. The downloaded versions can be the 2.7.12 and the 3.4.1 or the 3.5.2.

Step #2 – Solving addition, subtraction, multiplication and division problems

Let's say, you want to find the sum of 1,200 and 378. You just type 1200 + 378 and press 'enter'.

The answer will appear below your entry.

See the succeeding image.

You can easily perform subtraction (-), addition (+), multiplication (*) and division (/), by using the specified signs.

Simply type the number and the sign and press 'enter'.

If you don't want your answers in fraction numbers in your division, you can use a double slash (//).

Example:

Divide 5.678/2 = 2.839 (with decimal points)

5.678//2 = 2.0 (whole number)

See image below:

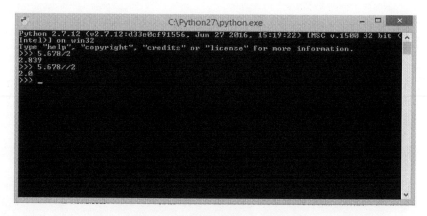

Step #3 – Solving numbers with exponents

Exponents are the 'power' by which numbers are raised. For example, 10^9, means that 10 is multiplied by itself 9 times; 10 is the base and 9 is the exponent. It could also be read: 10 raised to the power of 9, or 10 raised to the 9th power.

Hence $10^9 = 1000000000$

In Python, instead of multiplying 10, 9 times, you can use the double asterisk (**) as a short cut method.

Example:

10 ** 9 (enter the base number, and then the two asterisks and the exponent.)

See image below:

More examples:

$4^6 = 4*4*4*4*4*4$ will give 4096

This can be simplified by using two asterisks or stars.

$$4**6 = 4096$$

When you press enter, it will be giving the same answer. See image below.

Reminder:

In multiple signs, you must enclose (in parentheses), the solution that you want to be prioritized. Just like in your math problems, the chronological order of solving the problem is this: enclosed numbers are solved first, followed by exponents, then multiplication, then division, then addition and then subtraction.

Example:

$$5 + 6/5 + 2 - 7$$

If you want to prioritize the addition of 5 and 6, then enclose them in parentheses.

$$(5 + 6)/(5 + 5) - 7$$

In the problem above, (5 + 6) will be solved first, followed by (5+2), before 7 is subtracted.

Hence: $11/10 - 7 = -5.9$ or -6.

Notice that the answer will differ without the parentheses, so be sure to add them when needed.

$$5 + 6/5 + 2 - 7 = 1.2 \text{ or } 1$$

If you didn't prioritize any numbers, your Python will compute the problem based on the universal mathematical rule, stated in the above-mentioned reminder.

See image below:

```
                         C:\Python27\python.exe                    _  □  [x]
Python 2.7.12 (v2.7.12:d33e0cf91556, Jun 27 2016, 15:19:22) [MSC v.1500 32 bit (
Intel)] on win32
Type "help", "copyright", "credits" or "license" for more information.
>>> 4*4*4*4*4*4
4096
>>> 4**6
4096
>>> (5+6)/(5+2)-7
-6
>>> 5+6/5+2-7
1
>>> ▄
```

If you want to find out the functions available for math, simply type 'import math' (without the quotes) and press 'enter'.

The word 'math' will appear and then right click it to search (scroll down or up) for the different built-in functions or command words. Select the value you want and click 'enter', to access it.

Chapter 10: Using Variables and Assigning Values

Python makes use of variables. As previously discussed, variables can contain a string of words, an integer (number) or other items. Hence, they act as containers.

Step #1 – Specify the value of your variable.

In the example below, the value of your variable is 50.

Example:

Let's say you want your variable to be 50, you can enter this in your Python.

myVariable = 50

This is for Python version 3. The first letter is in the lower case and the first letter of the next words are in the upper case. This is termed the 'camel case declaration'.

You must remember that Python is case sensitive, so use the upper case and lower case letters whenever necessary.

myVariableTitle = 50

Step #2 – Press 'enter'.

After entering or assigning the value, you can press 'enter', and the value 50 will appear. This is your value.

You can make use of it in math operations to compute whatever you want to compute.

If your syntax is wrong, a syntax error appears in red ink, informing you of the mistake.

You can assign values to your variables by using the equal (=) sign. You have to name your variable before the equal sign and assign its values after the equal sign.

Examples:

name = "Billy"

surname = "Trump"

age = 45

height = 5

Your variables are: name, surname, age and height and the values assigned are: "Billy", "Trump", 45, and 5.

If you want to print your variables, you can create your statement or code this way:

```
name = "Billy"

surname = "Trump"

age = 45

height = 5


print name

print surname

print age

print height
```

See image below:

The original shell was used; thus, the variables are printed one by one by pressing your 'enter' tab/key.

Unlike if you open a 'New File', the results will be displayed all at once in a new shell:

```
>>>
>>> name="Billy"
>>> surname="Trump"
>>> age=45
>>> height=5
>>>
>>> print name
Billy
>>> print surname
Trump
>>> print age
45
>>> print height
5
```

If you decide to open a 'New File', the syntax/statement will appear this way:

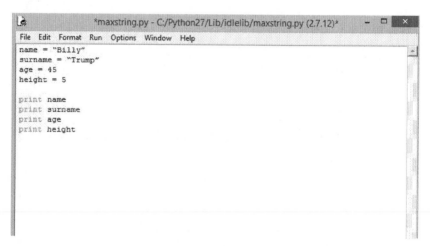

When you click 'Run', and then 'Run Module', the results will appear in a new shell:

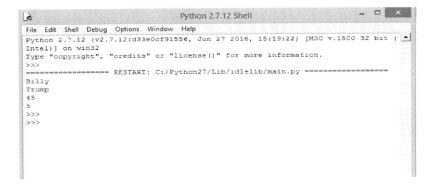

```
Python 2.7.12 Shell                                         – □ ✕
File  Edit  Shell  Debug  Options  Window  Help
Python 2.7.12 (v2.7.12:d33e0cf91556, Jun 27 2016, 15:19:22) [MSC v.1500 32 bit (
Intel)] on win32
Type "copyright", "credits" or "license()" for more information.
>>>
================= RESTART: C:/Python27/Lib/idlelib/main.py =================
Billy
Trump
45
5
>>>
>>>
```

It's smart to name your variables according to their objects/content, so you won't get confused accessing them later on.

As discussed, variables can contain names or integers, or different types of data. Male sure to separate them with commas.

For variables that you want to be printed literally in a string, don't include them inside braces [ ]. These will appear in the final output.

Multiple assignments for variables

You can also assign, simultaneously, a single value to multiple variables. Here's an example:

  Variables a, b, c, and d are all assigned to "1" memory location.

  a=b=c=d=1

Another example is where variables are assigned individual values:

311

a, b, c, d, = 1, 2, "Potter", 3

The value of a=1

The value of b=2

The value of c = "Potter"

And the value of d = 1

Take note again, that numbers or integers are not enclosed in quotes (quotation marks – "), while word-strings are enclosed in single, double quotes, or triple quotes. (' ', or " ", or """ """).

Chapter 11: Learning the Built-in Modules and Functions

Python contains built-in modules and functions that come with the program when you download it into your computer. Downloading the Python versions 2 and 3 in the same computer may not work, because some of their contents/functions are incompatible with each other, although they are both from Python.

The following are quick steps in accessing and learning these built-in modules and functions:

Step #1 – On your shell, type help('modules) and press 'enter'.

This command or function will provide all the modules of Python available in your downloaded Python.

When you press 'enter', it will take a few seconds for the list of modules to appear.

```
Python 2.7.12 Shell                                              –  □  ✕
File  Edit  Shell  Debug  Options  Window  Help
Python 2.7.12 (v2.7.12:d33e0cf91556, Jun 27 2016, 15:19:22) [MSC v.1500 32 bit (
Intel)] on win32
Type "copyright", "credits" or "license()" for more information.
>>> help('modules')

Please wait a moment while I gather a list of all available modules...

AutoComplete         _md5                ftplib              repr
AutoCompleteWindow   _msi                functools           rexec
AutoExpand           _multibytecodec     future_builtins     rfc822
BaseHTTPServer       _multiprocessing    gc                  rlcompleter
Bastion              _osx_support        genericpath         robotparser
Bindings             _pyio               getopt              rpc
CGIHTTPServer        _random             getpass             run
CallTipWindow        _sha                gettext             runpy
CallTips             _sha256             glob                sched
Canvas               _sha512             gzip                select
ClassBrowser         _socket             hashlib             sets
CodeContext          _sqlite3            heapq               setuptools
ColorDelegator       _sre                help                sgmllib
ConfigParser         _ssl                hmac                sha
Cookie               _strptime           hotshot             shelve
Debugger             _struct             htmlentitydefs      shlex
Delegator            _subprocess         htmllib             shutil
Dialog               _symtable           httplib             signal
DocXMLRPCServer      _testcapi           idle                site
EditorWindow         _threading_local    idle_test           smtpd
FileDialog           _tkinter            idlelib             smtplib
FileList             _warnings           idlever             sndhdr
FixTk                _weakref            ihooks              socket
```

Step #3 – Narrow down your search.

You can narrow down the search by being more specific. You can specify the type of module you want to find. Let's say, you want to access modules about 'profile', you can enter or type on your Python shell the following:

help("modules profile")

And then press 'enter'. The matching modules related to your designated search word will appear in your shell. See image below.

```
>>> help('modules profile')

Here is a list of matching modules.  Enter any module name to get more help.

_lsprof - Fast profiler
cProfile - Python interface for the 'lsprof' profiler.
hotshot - High-perfomance logging profiler, mostly written in C.
profile - Class for profiling Python code.
pstats - Class for printing reports on profiled python code.
test.profilee - Input for test_profile.py and test_cprofile.py.
test.test_cprofile - Test suite for the cProfile module.
test.test_profile - Test suite for the profile module.
test.test_sys_setprofile

>>>
```

The above image is only an example to demonstrate how to be more specific in your search for modules.

Step #4 – Find the built-in functions and modules.

You can access the Python built-in functions through your shell by typing the following:

dir(['__builtin__'])

See image below:

```
>>>
>>> dir(['__builtin__'])
['__add__', '__class__', '__contains__', '__delattr__', '__delitem__', '__delsli
ce__', '__doc__', '__eq__', '__format__', '__ge__', '__getattribute__', '__getit
em__', '__getslice__', '__gt__', '__hash__', '__iadd__', '__imul__', '__init__',
'__iter__', '__le__', '__len__', '__lt__', '__mul__', '__ne__', '__new__', '__r
educe__', '__reduce_ex__', '__repr__', '__reversed__', '__rmul__', '__setattr__'
, '__setitem__', '__setslice__', '__sizeof__', '__str__', '__subclasshook__', 'a
ppend', 'count', 'extend', 'index', 'insert', 'pop', 'remove', 'reverse', 'sort'
]
>>>
```

The different functions will appear on your Python shell. You can choose any of the functions you want to use.

You can also access the built-in functions or modules by importing them. This is done by opening your idle shell, and then typing:

import urllib

and then, type

dir(urllib)

When you press 'enter', all the Python modules will be displayed on your shell.

See image below:

```
Python 2.7.12 Shell                                              –  □  x

File  Edit  Shell  Debug  Options  Window  Help

Python 2.7.12 (v2.7.12:d33e0cf91556, Jun 27 2016, 15:19:22) [MSC v.1500 32 bit (
Intel)] on win32
Type "copyright", "credits" or "license()" for more information.
>>> import urllib
>>> dir(urllib)
['ContentTooShortError', 'FancyURLopener', 'MAXFTPCACHE', 'URLopener', '__all__'
, '__builtins__', '__doc__', '__file__', '__name__', '__package__', '__version__
', '__asciire', '_ftperrors', '_have_ssl', '_hexdig', '_hextochr', '_hostprog', '
_is_unicode', '_localhost', '_noheaders', '_nportprog', '_passwdprog', '_portpro
g', '_queryprog', '_safe_map', '_safe_quoters', '_tagprog', '_thishost', '_typep
rog', '_urlopener', '_userprog', '_valueprog', 'addbase', 'addclosehook', 'addin
fo', 'addinfourl', 'always_safe', 'base64', 'basejoin', 'c', 'ftpcache', 'ftperr
ors', 'ftpwrapper', 'getproxies', 'getproxies_environment', 'getproxies_registry
', 'i', 'localhost', 'noheaders', 'os', 'pathname2url', 'proxy_bypass', 'proxy_b
ypass_environment', 'proxy_bypass_registry', 'quote', 'quote_plus', 're', 'repor
thook', 'socket', 'splitattr', 'splithost', 'splitnport', 'splitpasswd', 'splitp
ort', 'splitquery', 'splittag', 'splittype', 'splituser', 'splitvalue', 'ssl', '
string', 'sys', 'test1', 'thishost', 'time', 'toBytes', 'unquote', 'unquote_plus
', 'unwrap', 'url2pathname', 'urlcleanup', 'urlencode', 'urlopen', 'urlretrieve'
]
>>> |
```

Step #5 – Find the uses of function words.

You can now explore the uses/functions of the function words displayed on your shell. That is, if you don't know the function of the word.

If you want to learn more about the uses of the function word 'max', you can use the help function by entering the following command:

helpmax

Press enter or execute. The use or functions of the word 'max' will be displayed on your shell, just like in the image below:

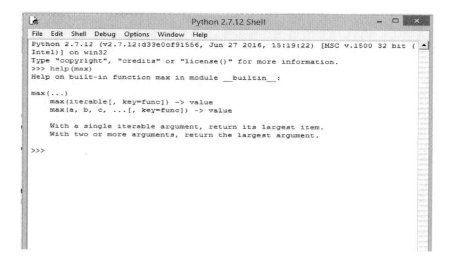

Based on the results in the image shown above, apparently, the function of 'max' is to show or display the largest item or largest (maximum) argument.

Therefore, if you want to know the largest item in a certain string, type max and then the values, and press enter.

The item with the highest value will be selected, just like the example below:

See image below:

```
                                                                        [×]
                    Python 2.7.12 Shell                         —  □  [×]
File  Edit  Shell  Debug  Options  Window  Help
Python 2.7.12 (v2.7.12:d33e0cf91556, Jun 27 2016, 15:19:22) [MSC v.1500 32 bit ( ▲
Intel)] on win32
Type "copyright", "credits" or "license()" for more information.
>>> help(max)
Help on built-in function max in module __builtin__:

max(...)
    max(iterable[, key=func]) -> value
    max(a, b, c, ...[, key=func]) -> value

    With a single iterable argument, return its largest item.
    With two or more arguments, return the largest argument.

>>> max(7,8,9,10)
10
>>> max(3,6,9,11)
11
>>> |
```

As shown above, the highest value of the first set is 10, and
the second is 11.

Step #5 - Access the Python modules and built-in functions from your downloaded file.

Another alternative is to access the different Python
functions from the files that you have saved.

Remember, if your Python syntax or statement is wrong,
the words will be colored red. So, it's easy to detect errors
in your commands or statements.

Chapter 12: Creating, Saving and Running Python Files

You can create and save your Python files, so you can easily access and run them, whenever you need them. There are standard data types used in Python that you have to learn; these are: strings, lists, numbers, tuples and the dictionary.

But how do you create, save and run your own files?

Here's how:

Step #1 – Open your Python shell.

As instructed in the earlier chapter, after you have downloaded and saved the Python program in your computer/device, you can open your Python shell by clicking your saved Python and click IDLE (for Python version 3) or follow the instructions for version 2 as discussed in chapter 7.

Step #2 – Click on the 'File' menu of your shell.

At the left, the uppermost portion of your Python shell, click the 'File' menu. The down scroll options will appear. Click on 'New File'. See image below:

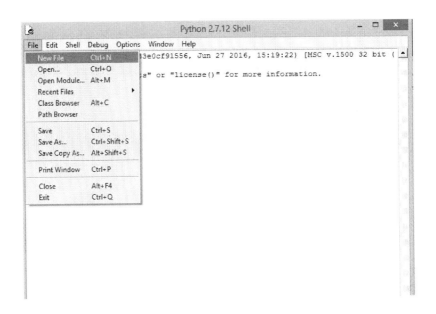

Step #3 – Create your 'New File'.

When you click on the 'New File' option, a blank box will appear. See image below:

The new box is where you can create your file for saving. If you have noticed, the file is still untitled because you will be assigning the title before you can save it. You may save the file first before proceeding, or proceed to write your Python statement/code before saving.

Write your file.

For example, you want to create a file to provide the maximum or largest value of your variables (a, b, c, d), you can enter in your new file in the following manner:

a=int(input("Please enter 1st number"))

b=int(input("Please enter 2nd number"))

c=int(input("Please enter 3rd number"))

d=int(input("Please enter 4th number"))

print (max(a,b,c,d))

See image below:

```
*math1.py - C:/Python27/math1.py (2.7.12)*
File  Edit  Format  Run  Options  Window  Help
a=int(input("Please enter 1st number"))
b=int(input("Please enter 2nd number"))
c=int(input("Please enter 3rd number"))
d=int(input("Please enter 4th number"))

print (max(a,b,c,d))
```

Make sure you enter the correct items and have used the necessary quotes and parentheses.

Any error in the signs, indentations, and quotes in your statement will yield errors.

Python won't be able to execute your command, and says so in red ink.

Step #4 – Save your New File.

You can save your 'New File' before writing it. Just access the 'File' menu, and choose 'Save As'.

See image below:

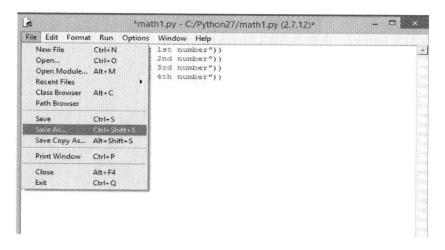

When you click on the 'Save As' option, a box will appear allowing you to select the name of your file, and where you want to save your file. Ascertain that your file is with the suffix .py.

Let's say you want to name your file math1. Type the name on the provided box, and press 'Save'. See image below:

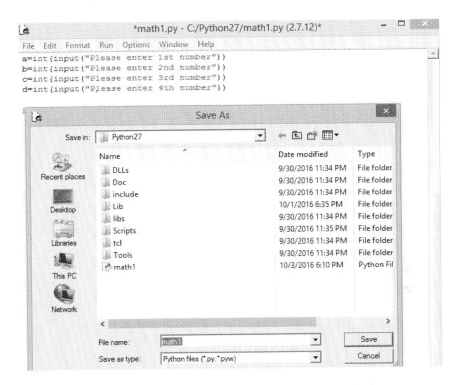

Step #5 – Run your 'New File' (math 1) or module.

You can now run your 'New File' by clicking on the 'Run' option, or key in F5 on your computer's keypads. See image below:

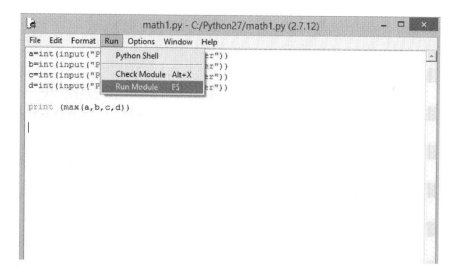

When you click on the 'Run Module' option, a new shell will appear. You can now enter your variables or values. See image below:

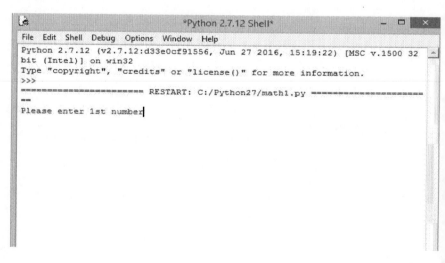

Test your file if it's working by providing the values required. Let's say the values of your items - a, b, c, and d - are 1356, 1827, 1359 and 1836. When you press 'enter', the value 1836 will appear, because it is the largest or highest value. See image below.

Of course, you can add more statements/codes, if you wish. This is just an example of how to create and save your Python file.

You can add another item/command, ("Please press enter to exit"), to provide easier access. Save your file again. See image below.

```
math1.py - C:/Python27/math1.py (2.7.12)                    –  □  ✕
File  Edit  Format  Run  Options  Window  Help
a=int(input("Please enter 1st number"))
b=int(input("Please enter 2nd number"))
c=int(input("Please enter 3rd number"))
d=int(input("Please enter 4th number"))

print (max(a,b,c,d))

input("Please press enter to exit")
```

Remember to ALWAYS save any changes you made in your Python statement, and double check that your saved file is a .py file.

Take note that Python doesn't compile your programs, you have to run them directly.

Deleting files

To delete files, use the key 'del'.

Example:

myname="Lincoln"

myage=20

del myname

This will delete your variable 'myname', and whatever is specified in your command or code.

You can remove as many variables as you please. Don't worry, you can always create new files, if you want to.

Chapter 13: Utilizing User-Defined Functions

User-defined functions often come to play when creating your Python codes. These functions can be used when you want a task or code done repeatedly. Functions can also help in maintaining your codes.

Keep in mind that you also have your built-in functions, which you can easily 'call', whenever you need them. However, you can create and utilize your own user-defined functions.

Step #1 – Use a keyword to define a function.

The function should be defined first making use of the word 'def', and then the name of its function.

When you want to define a function, you can use the general code below:

```
def functionname (arg1, arg2, arg3)

        statement1

        statement2

        statement3
```

Press 'enter' twice to access results.

Take note: arg stands for argument.

Example:

You are an employer, and you want to print the numbers (num) of your employees, thus, you defined 'employee' as the name of your file.

def employee(num)

print ("num")

See image below:

```
Python 2.7.12 Shell
File  Edit  Shell  Debug  Options  Window  Help
Python 2.7.12 (v2.7.12:d33e0cf91556, Jun 27 2016, 15:19:22) [MSC v.1500 32 bit (
Intel)] on win32
Type "copyright", "credits" or "license()" for more information.
>>>
>>> def employee(num) :
        print ('employee', num)
```

When you press enter, and input a number, the function will keep going until you decide to stop. So, the function can work repetitively. See image below:

```
Python 2.7.12 Shell
File  Edit  Shell  Debug  Options  Window  Help
Python 2.7.12 (v2.7.12:d33e0cf91556, Jun 27 2016, 15:19:22) [MSC v.1500 3:
Intel)] on win32
Type "copyright", "credits" or "license()" for more information.
>>>
>>> def employee(num) :
        print ('employee', num)

>>> employee (101)
('employee', 101)
>>>
>>> employee (301)
('employee', 301)
```

You can also create the Python syntax this way:

331

```
def employee(num)

    print 'employee', num
```

Press 'enter' twice and then you can begin entering the numbers. The program will print it ad infinitum. See image below:

Functions can have no arguments, or have a couple of arguments. The arguments can be numbers, or strings.

You can also make use of the keyword 'return' to 'return' results (the 'return' key indicates that answers to the computation specified will be 'returned' – (displayed in the results).

Example:

If you want to obtain the average of the grades of students in 4 subjects, you can create the code this way: You can use this code for as long as you don't exit the shell. If you want to save it, you can create a New File so you could save it.

def grades(a,b,c,d) :

return ((a+b+c+d)/4)

See image below:

```
Python 2.7.12 Shell                                               — ☐ ✕
File  Edit  Shell  Debug  Options  Window  Help
Python 2.7.12 (v2.7.12:d33e0cf91556, Jun 27 2016, 15:19:22) [MSC v.1500 32 bit (
Intel)] on win32
Type "copyright", "credits" or "license()" for more information.
>>>
>>> def grades(a,b,c,d) :
        return ((a+b+c+d)/4)

>>>
```

When you, or the student enters his grades following the syntax/statement, the 'return' results would be the computed value already. See image below:

```
Python 2.7.12 Shell
File  Edit  Shell  Debug  Options  Window  Help
Python 2.7.12 (v2.7.12:d33e0cf91556, Jun 27 2016, 15:19:22) [MSC v.15
Intel)] on win32
Type "copyright", "credits" or "license()" for more information.
>>>
>>> def grades(a,b,c,d) :
        return ((a+b+c+d)/4)

>>>
>>> grades(80,79,81,84)
81
>>> grades(77,85,87,77)
81
>>> grades(90,88,86,85)
87
>>> grades(88,80,79,85)
83
>>> |
```

The student has to type in the shell, after the arrows (>>>), following the given format:

grades(80,90,85,75)

Through this method, you can compute the grades of your students- ad infinitum.

Take note that 'return' results are different from 'return' statements. Refer to the chapter involved.

Keep in mind that you have first to define (def) the function, before your code can work, and print the results.

Remember to add the colon (:) after your def statement. You must also separate the arguments by commas.

In default parameters, the originally assigned value is printed, when the user doesn't enter any value.

In multiple parameters, an asterisk (*) can be used to indicate this.

Be adventurous and discover the joy of knowing how to make your codes work with Python.

Chapter 14: How to Use and Define a Class

Classes, as defined earlier, are data that contain objects that are related to each other. The functions that are applied to these classes are also related to each other.

The keyword 'self' is a sparring partner for class data because it's used in creating your class statements.

For classes to be used correctly, it's important to create correct Python statements and syntax.

How do you use your classes? Here's how.

For example, you're the 'big boss' of a company, and you want to compile the personal information of your employees, you can create a Python class code to do this.

Step #1 – Use the 'class' keyword.

Open a New File and save it. Use the 'class' keyword in introducing your class code.

Step #2 – Add the name of your 'class'.

Add the name of your class (file name). Since the data is the personal information of your employees, you may want to name it - PersonnelInfo .

Step #3 – Add the colon at the end of the first statement.

Hence, it will appear this way: class PersonnelInfo :

Step #4 – Define your variables

You have to define or assign variables to your data. You need to use the word 'self' to indicate that the code is referring to the class.

In general, a class statement appears this way:

class ClassName :

<statement-1>

.

.

.

<statement – last>

Step #5 – Run your module.

See image below:

e

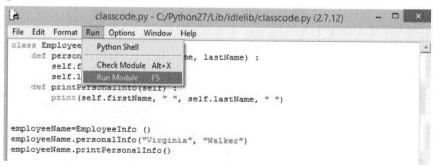

Two types of class object operations

1. **Class instantiation** – this type utilizes function notations in calling a class object. A special method, (double underscore)__init__(double underscore) (

) (bracket), can be defined by a class. __init__is called a class constructor and it's used to initialize (init) a value. Python uses this keyword to indicate (initialization).

Example:

```
def __init__self :

    self.data = [ ]
```

The class instantiation using the __init__ ( ) method, automatically raises __init__( ) for the newly formed class instance.

Example:

```
class EmployeeInfo:

    def __init__ (self) :

        print ("Employee Information Data")

        def personalInfo(self, firstName, lastName) :

        self.firstName=firstName

         self.lastName=lastName

    def printPersonalInfo(self) :

        print(self.firstName, " ", self.lastName, " ")


employeeName=EmployeeInfo ()

employeeName.personalInfo("Virginia", "Walker")

employeeName.printPersonalInfo()
```

See image below:

```
*classcode.py - C:/Python27/Lib/idlelib/classcode.py (2.7.12)*
File  Edit  Format  Run  Options  Window  Help
class EmployeeInfo:
    def __init__ (self) :
        print ("Employee Information Data.")
    def personalInfo(self, firstName, lastName) :
        self.firstName=firstName
        self.lastName=lastName
    def printPersonalInfo(self) :
        print(self.firstName, ' ', self.lastName, ' ')


employeeName=EmployeeInfo ()
employeeName.personalInfo('Virginia', 'Walker')
employeeName.printPersonalInfo()
```

Save and click 'Run', and then 'Run Module'.

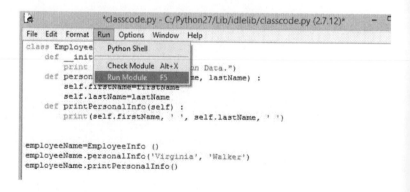

When you click 'Run Module', a new shell will be opened with this image:

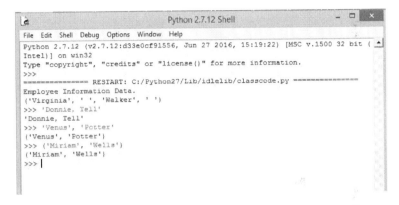

You can now enter your employees' names. See image below.

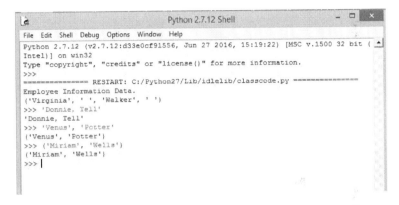

We have also what we call 'destructors' represented by the Python keyword ___del___( ): (double underscore + del + double underscore + brackets + colon.

This function will destroy or delete specified data or acts as a trash can for the data. Just like ___init___, it automatically functions even without 'calling' it out.

Example: (We'll use the same example above, but with the ___del___ function.)

```python
class EmployeeInfo:

    def __init__ (self) :

        print ("Employee Information Data.")

    def __del__ (self) :

        print ("Employee Information Data is discontinued")

    def personalInfo(self, firstName, lastName) :

        self.firstName=firstName

        self.lastName=lastName

    def printPersonalInfo(self) :

        print(self.firstName, ' ', self.lastName, ' ')


employeeName=EmployeeInfo ( )

employeeName.personalInfo('Virginia', 'Walker')

employeeName.printPersonalInfo( )
```

See image below:

```
*classcode.py - C:/Python27/Lib/idlelib/classcode.py (2.7.12)*
File  Edit  Format  Run  Options  Window  Help
class EmployeeInfo:
    def __init__ (self) :
        print ("Employee Information Data.")
    def __del__ (self) :
        print ("Employee Information Data is discontinued")
    def personalInfo(self, firstName, lastName) :
        self.firstName=firstName
        self.lastName=lastName
    def printPersonalInfo(self) :
        print(self.firstName, ' ', self.lastName, ' ')


employeeName=EmployeeInfo ()
employeeName.personalInfo('Virginia', 'Walker')
employeeName.printPersonalInfo()
```

If you use the del keyword in the object or instance,
for example:

Adding employeeName.__del__ ( )

The resources or employees' name will be deleted or
destroyed.

See image below:

```
*classcode.py - C:/Python27/Lib/idlelib/classcode.py (2.7.12)*
File  Edit  Format  Run  Options  Window  Help
class employeeInfo:
    def __init__ (self) :
        print ("Employee Information Data.")
    def __del__ (self) :
        print ("Employee Information Data is discontinued")
    def personalInfo(self, firstName, lastName) :
        self.firstName=firstName
        self.lastName=lastName
    def printPersonalInfo(self) :
        print(self.firstName, ' ', self.lastName, ' ')


employeeName=EmployeeInfo ()
employeeName.personalInfo('Virginia', 'Walker')
employeeName.printPersonalInfo()
employeeName.__del__()
```

When you click 'Run', and then 'Run Module', a new shell will open. See image below:

```
Python 2.7.12 Shell
File  Edit  Shell  Debug  Options  Window  Help
Python 2.7.12 (v2.7.12:d33e0cf91556, Jun 27 2016, 15:19:22) [MSC v.1500 32 bit (
Intel)] on win32
Type "copyright", "credits" or "license()" for more information.
>>>
=============== RESTART: C:/Python27/Lib/idlelib/classcode.py ===============
Employee Information Data.
('Virginia', ' ', 'Walker', ' ')
Employee Information Data is discontinued
>>>
```

Example #2: (for __init__)

class Employee :

        def __init__ (self, name, address) :

            self.name=name

            self.address=address

print (employee.name)

print (employee.address)

See image below:

```
init1.py - C/Python27/init1.py (2.7.12)
File  Edit  Format  Run  Options  Window  Help
class Employee :

    def __init__(self, name, address):
        self.name=name
        self.address=address


employee = Employee("Virginia Walker", "Apt. G, Reed Avenue, Cheyenne, Wyoming")


print(employee.name)
print(employee.address)
```

When you click 'Run', and then 'Run Module', another Python shell will open, printing the results. See image below:

You can edit your code to produce results that are in congruence with your preferences. Isn't it fun?

Reminders:

For each definition, a colon (:) is added at the end of the statement.

'self' is always included in each member function, even if there are no arguments. Example of arguments are those values found inside the parentheses (self, firstName, LastName).

Single quotes or double quotes can be used with the arguments.

The constructor and destructor can contain arguments other than self. You can include any arguments you want. Example of arguments is (self, firstName, lastName). Make sure though that your __init__ arguments are included in the instances or objects' statements that come after the 'def'.

2. **Attribute references** – this type uses the 'object.name' of common Python syntax. Whenever you define a function of a class always passes an argument on 'self'. This is because the 'self' is pointing to the class.

Example:

We will be using the same code above – without the __init__ function. If you want the data about your employees, you can create your code this way:

```
class EmployeeInfo:

    def personalInfo(self, firstName, lastName) :

        self.firstName=firstName

        self.lastName=lastName

    def printPersonalInfo(self) :

        print(self.firstName, " ", self.lastName, " ")


employeeName=EmployeeInfo ()

employeeName.personalInfo("Virginia", "Walker")
```

employeeName.printPersonalInfo()

See image below:

```
classcode.py - C:/Python27/Lib/idlelib/classcode.py (2.7.12)
File  Edit  Format  Run  Options  Window  Help
class EmployeeInfo:
    def personalInfo(self, firstName, lastName) :
        self.firstName=firstName
        self.lastName=lastName
    def printPersonalInfo(self) :
        print(self.firstName, " ", self.lastName, " ")


employeeName=EmployeeInfo ()
employeeName.personalInfo("Virginia", "Walker")
employeeName.printPersonalInfo()
```

In the example above, in each definition (def) of a class, 'self' is always added for every function of the class. Notice also the indentations for the 'def' statements.

The following entries are not indented because the statements are not part of the definition of the class, but they are objects, or instances of the class.

employeeName=EmployeeInfo ( )

employeeName.personalInfo("Virginia", "Walker")

employeeName.printPersonalInfo ( )

If you run the class code above, this would appear in your Python shell:

```
Python 2.7.12 Shell

File  Edit  Shell  Debug  Options  Window  Help

Python 2.7.12 (v2.7.12:d33e0cf91556, Jun 27 2016, 15:19:22) [MSC v.1500 32 bit (
Intel)] on win32
Type "copyright", "credits" or "license()" for more information.
>>>
=============== RESTART: C:/Python27/Lib/idlelib/classcode.py ===============
('Virginia', ' ', 'Walker', ' ')
>>>
```

Tweak the codes and see what happens. Curiosity doesn't always kill the cat.

Chapter 15: Creating & Accessing Your Python Dictionary

Python dictionaries are usually enclosed by curly brackets { }. However, when accessing and assigning values, square brackets [ ] are used.

To create your own dictionary, you can start with the key 'dict':

> dict{ }
>
> dict ['filename'] = ['values']

Example:

> dict{ }
>
> dict['name'] = "My name is Billy."

When you print this by running the module with this function:

> print dict['name']

```
*dict1.py - C:/Python27/Lib/idlelib/dict1.py (2.7.12)*
File   Edit   Format   Run   Options   Window   Help

dict = {}
dict['name'] = "My name is Billy."

print dict['name']
```

The results will appear in a new shell/box – all the values of your dict['name'] will be printed.

See image below:

```
Python 2.7.12 Shell
File   Edit   Shell   Debug   Options   Window   Help
Python 2.7.12 (v2.7.12:d33e0cf91556, Jun 27 2016, 15:19:22) [MSC v.1500 32 bit (
Intel)] on win32
Type "copyright", "credits" or "license()" for more information.
>>>
================ RESTART: C:/Python27/Lib/idlelib/dict1.py ================
My name is Billy.
>>>
>>> |
```

You could also assign numbers as your dictionary's name, such as dict[1], and so forth. Make sure you have assigned values to your dictionary file.

Example:

> dict[1] = "My age is 25."

You can print your dict[1], by using: print dict[1], to display its values/content. See image below:

When you run the module, this will be the result:

Notice that all the values of dict1 have been printed in the results.

If you want to print the complete dictionary, you can use this statement:

print tinydict

But there should be values assigned to your tinydict, or your results will show errors.

See image below:

```
tinydict.py - C:/Python27/Lib/idlelib/tinydict.py (2.7.12)
File  Edit  Format  Run  Options  Window  Help
dict = {}

tinydict={'student': 'Ted', 'grade': 86, 'college': 'engineering'}

print tinydict
```

After you click 'Run', and then 'Run Module', a new shell will appear with results like the image below:

```
Python 2.7.12 Shell
File  Edit  Shell  Debug  Options  Window  Help
Python 2.7.12 (v2.7.12:d33e0cf91556, Jun 27 2016, 15:19:22) [MSC v.1500 32 bit (
Intel)] on win32
Type "copyright", "credits" or "license()" for more information.
>>>
================ RESTART: C:/Python27/Lib/idlelib/tinydict.py ================
{'grade': 86, 'college': 'engineering', 'student': 'Ted'}
>>>
>>>
```

You can also print all the values of your tinydict, by using this statement or code:

> print tinydict.values()

The results below will appear:

```
>>>
>>> print tinydict.values()
[86, 'engineering', 'Ted']
>>>
>>>
>>> |
```

Notice that there are >>> symbols in this shell. This is because the original shell was used without opening a 'New File'.

If you want to print the keys of your tinydict, you can use this statement:

print tinydict.keys()

```
>>>
>>>
>>> print tinydict.keys()|
```

When you press 'enter' or execute, the results will be this:

```
>>>
>>> print tinydict.keys()
['grade', 'college', 'student']
>>>
>>>
>>> |
```

All the keys are printed in the results. Often, the results don't come in the order that it was presented/written in the tinydict.

Reminder:

If you have opted to create a 'New File', click the 'Run', and the 'Run Module'. If not, just press 'enter' and the results will be printed promptly in the same Python shell.

The advantage of creating a 'New File', however, is that you can edit the file without difficulty. This is because when you press the 'enter' key it does not execute the code, not until you click the 'Run' and 'Run Module' menu on the New File's shell, itself.

Accessing Values from a Python Dictionary:

You can access values from a Python dictionary by entering the correct code. To access values, you can use the square brackets and the keyword (key).

In the dictionary, the keyword is separated from its value by a colon (:), and the values are separated by commas, and all items are enclosed in curly braces { }.

Example:

dict={'student': 'White', 'gender': 'female'}

print "dict['student']: ", dict['student']

print "dict['gender']; ", dict['gender']

See image below:

```
┌─────────────────────────────────────────────────────────────┐
│ ▐ᴸᵉ                    *Untitled*                    ─  □  ▮ │
├─────────────────────────────────────────────────────────────┤
│ File  Edit  Format  Run  Options  Window  Help              │
│                                                              │
│ dict={'student':'White', 'gender':'female'}                 │
│                                                              │
│ print "dict['student']: " , dict['student']                 │
│ print "dict['gender']: "  , dict['gender']                  │
│ |                                                            │
└─────────────────────────────────────────────────────────────┘
```

Before you can access this though, the file should have been saved in your device.

Chapter 16: Creating and Combining Strings

Writing your strings properly for your codes can help you significantly in obtaining correct results.

These are the steps:

Step #1 – Open a 'New File.'

From your shell, open a 'New File,' as instructed in the previous chapter. On this box, you can now create your string.

As previously defined, strings can contain variable numbers or words.

Step #2 – Identify your variables.

Let's say you have chosen three variables, a, b, and c. You can then assign a string to each of the variables before printing them.

Example:

a=('This is a single quoted string.')

b=("This is a double quoted string.")

c=("""This is a triple quoted string.""")

print (a)

print (b)

print (c)

See the example of composing and assigning values to your variables, using strings, demonstrated in the image below:

Step #3 – Save your New File.

Again, name and 'Save As' your 'New File' where you want it to be. In this case, the file is named string1 and saved in the Python file. Remember to save every time you make changes. See image below.

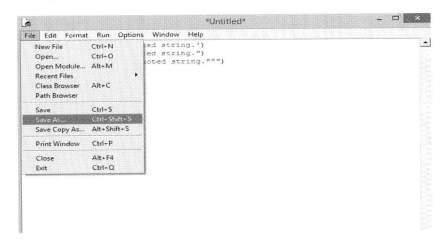

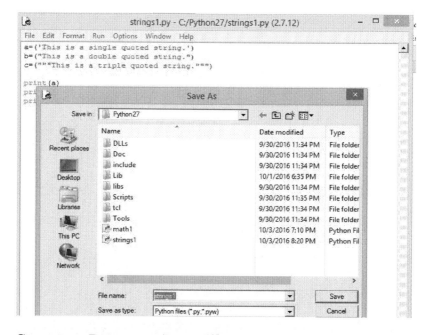

Step #4 – Run your 'New File'.

You can now run your new Python file by clicking 'Run" and then 'Run Module', or simply key in F5. See image below:

Step #5 – Use your new module (strings 1)

Go back to your Python shell and import your 'New File', strings1, so you can use it. Simply type: import strings1, and then press 'enter'. The results will appear, with your strings displayed quickly.

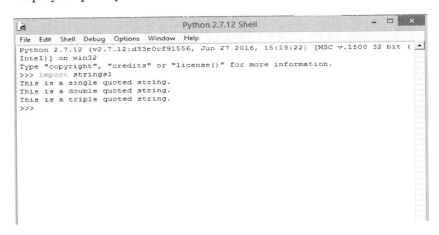

Let's say you have already assigned the values of string 'a' as 'Remember.' and your string 'b' as "Yesterday and

Tomorrow.", you have to save the changes you made to strings1, by clicking 'Save'.

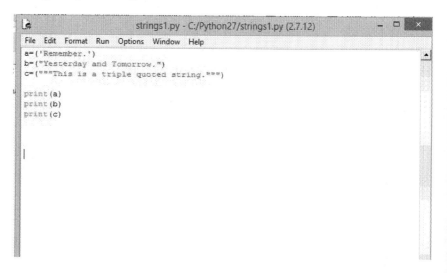

If you want to combine string 'a' and string 'b', you can go back to your Python shell and import strings1, before combining them.

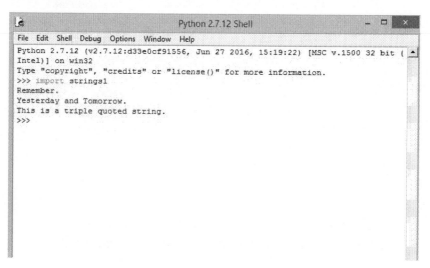

Now, you can combine them, by using the statement or command:

> print (a + b),

and then press 'enter'.

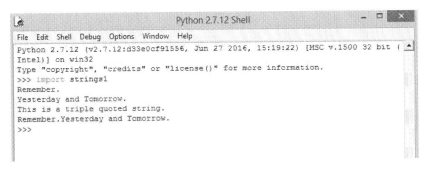

You can do this on your strings1 file itself or in the Python shell. This was done in the file itself, so the combined strings are already displayed when strings1 was imported.

There are other functions that you can take advantage of, such as printing any of the strings repeatedly.

If you want to print string 'b' repeatedly (example: 200 times), you can use the statement: print(b asterisk 200).

> print (b * 200)

This will print your 'b' string = "Yesterday and Tomorrow." 200 times. The long method is using the command:

print (b + b + b ... (until it reaches 200), which is a tedious task.

You can enter this function or command in your strings1 file, and then go back to your Python shell and import strings1.

See image below.

The results will be displayed in your shell, when the file (strings1) is imported. See image below.

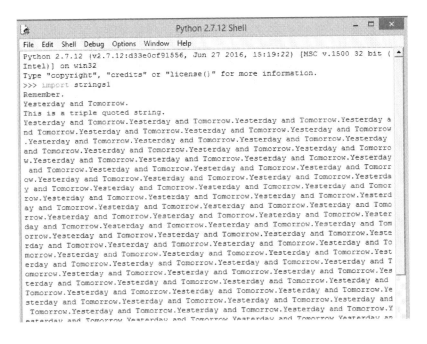

You can also click 'Run' in your strings1 file to show the results. See image below:

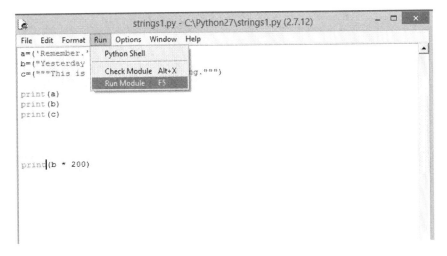

When you click on the 'Run Module' or F5, the same results will appear quickly. See image below:

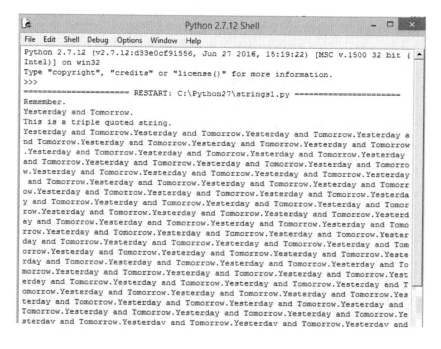

Reminders:

Generally, you cannot combine arguments that are different. For example, integers (numbers) and strings (words).

What you can do is to convert your integer into a word-string by using the prefix, 'str'.

You can create a New File to edit you string1 file with a new string.

In this case, I decided to modify the string1 file. Remember always to save your file, every time you edit or create a new file.

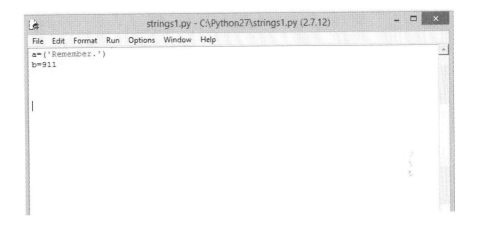

Take note that integers don't need any parentheses. You cannot add string literals (words) and numbers in one string, so you have to convert the number to a string first, by the key function: str(b).

Next, add 'a' and 'b' with the function/command +:

```
print(a + str(b))
```

Don't forget to enclose your argument in parentheses.

See image below:

```
*strings1.py - C:\Python27\strings1.py (2.7.12)*
File  Edit  Format  Run  Options  Window  Help
a=('Remember.')
b=911


print(a + str(b))
|
```

Click 'Save', and then click 'Run', and then 'Run Module'.

The combination of arguments 'a' and 'b' will appear, which is:

Remember. 911

See image below:

```
Python 2.7.12 Shell
File  Edit  Shell  Debug  Options  Window  Help
Python 2.7.12 (v2.7.12:d33e0cf91556, Jun 27 2016, 15:19:22) [MSC v.1500 32 bit (
Intel)] on win32
Type "copyright", "credits" or "license()" for more information.
>>>
===================== RESTART: C:\Python27\strings1.py =====================
Remember.911
>>> |
```

A more specific example is this.

You want to create a personal file about your clients. So, you click on 'File', and then 'New File', just like the previous steps previously discussed.

Let's say you have two arguments, 'Names' and 'Ages', that you would like to combine in your file.

The existing data you have are:

Names: Potter Richard, Walker Henry, Fell Don, Dean James

Ages: 20, 34, 41, 32

See image below:

So, if you want to combine the 'Names' and the 'Ages' strings, your code would be:

print (Names + Ages)

Make sure you save, after entering your code. Enclose each entry with quotes, and separate each entry with a comma. Use parentheses (brackets) for word strings, and no parentheses or quotes for integers (numbers). Don't forget the equal sign when assigning your arguments.

Example:

Names = ("Potter Richard", "Walker Henry", "Fell Don", "Dean James")

Ages = 20, 34, 41, 32

print (Names + Ages)

See image below:

Now, save. Click 'Run', and 'Run Module'. See image below:

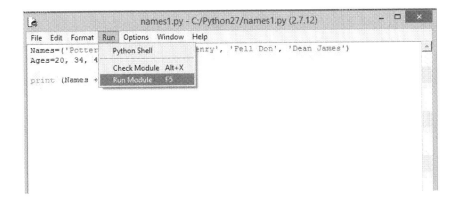

After you had clicked 'Run Module', a new Python shell will appear displaying the results of your code.

See image below:

In this instance, you don't need to create a name string for your integers.

Using the 'join; ( ) key.

You can also use the key, 'join', to combine strings.

Example:

parts=['Richard', 'Potter', 'Probationary']

' '.join(parts)

'Richard Potter Probationary'

' , ' .join(parts)

'Richard, Potter, Probationary'

' ' .join(parts)

'Richard Potter Probationary'

See image below:

```
>>>
>>> parts=['Richard', 'Potter', 'Probationary']
>>> ' '.join(parts)
'Richard Potter Probationary'
>>> ' , ' .join(parts)
'Richard , Potter , Probationary'
>>> ' ' .join(parts)
'Richard Potter Probationary'
>>>
```

These are all methods in creating and combining strings.

I hope you can now create your own strings and combine them in your Python shell. Remember is the key functions (+) and 'join'( ).

Chapter 17: Accessing and Updating Strings

Python strings are one of the most popular methods in creating and maintaining codes. They are also very simple to create, as you have read in the previous chapter.

You can access your strings promptly by using the keywords (key) 'import'.

In our examples in the previous chapter, we have saved 'names1' and 'strings1'.

When you need to access them, you can simply import them using your Python shell. Simply type:

import names1,

And then press 'enter'.

See image below:

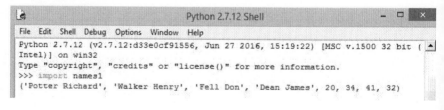

Of course, you must save your files before you could access them.

For substrings, you can slice through them by using brackets. Please refer to the chapter about slicing lists because the instructions are similar.

Anyway, here's one example of accessing your substrings. Let's say your strings are these:

> var1="Welcome to My World."

> var2="Clinical Chemistry"

And you want to get the substrings 1:4 for var1, and the substrings 1:3 for var2. You can enter your statement/code this way: (You can open a 'New File' to do this. Click on 'File', and then 'New File'. Please refer to the chapter on creating files).

Example:

> var1="Welcome to My World."

> var2="Clinical Chemistry"

> print "var1[1:4]: ",var1[1:4]

> print "var2[1:3]: ",var2[1:3]

See image below:

```
*Untitled*
File  Edit  Format  Run  Options  Window  Help
var1="Welcome to My World."
var2="Clinical Chemistry"


print "var1[1:4]: ",var1[1:4]
print "var2[1:3]: ",var2[1:3]
```

Keep in mind that just like in your indexes, each letter is assigned a number, with the number starting from o and then onwards.

Hence, for the first variable [var1], letter W=0; letter e = 1, and so forth. For the second variable [var2], the first letter C is equivalent to 0 and then so forth.

When you press 'Run', and then 'Run Module', on your keypads, a new shell will appear with these results. See image below:

```
Python 2.7.12 Shell
File  Edit  Shell  Debug  Options  Window  Help
Python 2.7.12 (v2.7.12:d33e0cf91556, Jun 27 2016, 15:19:22) [MSC v.1500 32 bit (
Intel)] on win32
Type "copyright", "credits" or "license()" for more information.
>>>
=============== RESTART: C:/Python27/Lib/idlelib/edit var1.py ===============
var1[1:4]:  elc
var2[1:3]:  li
>>>
```

If you noticed, only the letters that correspond to the numbers are printed - 'elc' from the original word, 'Welcome to My World'.

W=0,

e= 1,

l=2,

c=3,

o=4,

m=5,

e=6

and so on

Only the letters 'elc' were accessed. As stated in rule #4 is not included in the results (refer to chapter on slicing lists), when you access indexes or strings.

Likewise, with var2, only 'li' was accessed because of the specified numbers – 1:3; in these examples the colon stands for 'to', and #3 is not included in the results. However, only 1 to 2 letters will appear, so the result printed is 'li', from the original word, 'Clinical Chemistry'.

C=0,

l=1,

i=2,

n=3,

i=4,

c=5,

a=6,

l=7

and so on

Updating your strings

You can update your strings quickly by indicating what updates you want to do. Let's say you want to add the words "Welcome" from your var1 with "Chemistry" from var2, here's how your code/statement would appear:

Example:

var1="Welcome to My World."

print "Updated String :- ", var1[:8] + 'Chemistry'

See image below:

```
update1.py - C:/Python27/Lib/idlelib/update1.py (2.7.12)         -  □  ×
File  Edit  Format  Run  Options  Window  Help
var1="Welcome to My World."

print "Updated String :- ", var1[ :8] + 'Chemistry'
```

When you click 'Run', and then 'Run Module', a new shell will appear with the results:

It's preferable to open a 'New File' every time you input new data, than typing in the original shell, because some beginners may find the results confusing because of the >>> signs. You can also save the 'New File' easily.

See image below:

But if you don't find this confusing, you may opt not to open a 'New File', and type in the new Python shell instead.

See image below:

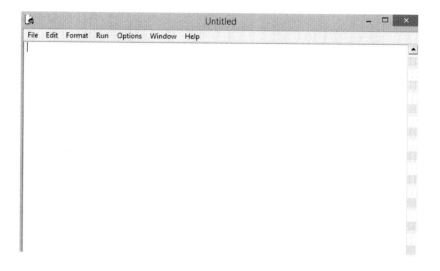

Chapter 18: Built-in Functions to Format Strings

Python has built-in keys or functions to format your strings. You can access them from your built-in directory.

Here are some of the most common built-in methods:

1. **capitalize ( )**

   This key/function capitalizes the first letter of the string.

   Example:

   str = "my name is unknown.";

   print "str.capitalize( ) : ", str.capitalize( )

   See image below:

When you click 'Run' and 'Run Module', the results will appear in a new shell:

```
Python 2.7.12 Shell                                    - □

File  Edit  Shell  Debug  Options  Window  Help
Python 2.7.12 (v2.7.12:d33e0cf91556, Jun 27 2016, 15:19:22) [MSC v.1500 32 bit (
Intel)] on win32
Type "copyright", "credits" or "license()" for more information.
>>>
==================== RESTART: C:/Python27/Lib/idlelib/7.py ====================
str.capitalize() :  My name is unknown.
>>>
>>>
```

As you can see in the resulting shell, the first letter (m) in the string is already capitalized (M).

2. count ( ) or count(string, beg=0, end=len(string))

Its function is to count the frequency of the occurrence of the specified string, starting from the beginning to the end of the string indexes, or substring indexes.

Example:

str = "my name is unknown.";

sub = "n";

print "str.count(sub, 3, 10) : ", str.count(sub, 3, 10)

sub = "unknown";

print "str.count(sub) : ", str.count(sub)

See image below:

```
*ex count2.py - C:/Python27/Lib/idlelib/ex count2.py (2.7.12)*
File  Edit  Format  Run  Options  Window  Help
str = "my name is unknown.";

sub = "n";
print "str.count(sub, 3, 10) : ", str.count(sub, 3, 10)
sub = "unknown";
print "str.count(sub) : ", str.count(sub)
```

When you click 'Run', and then 'Run Module', the results will appear this way:

```
Python 2.7.12 Shell
File  Edit  Shell  Debug  Options  Window  Help
Python 2.7.12 (v2.7.12:d33e0cf91556, Jun 27 2016, 15:19:22) [MSC v.1500 32 bit (
Intel)] on win32
Type "copyright", "credits" or "license()" for more information.
>>>
=============== RESTART: C:/Python27/Lib/idlelib/ex count2.py ===============
str.count(sub, 3, 10) :  1
str.count(sub) :  1
>>>
```

This means there's only 1 "n" letter counted, and 1 'unknown' word counted in the specified strings.

3. center () or center (width, fillchar)

This key/function allows your string to be centered, if indicated, depending on the total of the width columns. The general syntax is this.

Example:

str.center(width[, fillchar])

width – indicates the total width of the string.

fillchar – indicates the filler character.

Example:

str = "My name is unknown.";

print "str.center(40, 'a') : ", str.center(40, 'a')

See image below:

```
centerstring.py - C:/Python27/Lib/idlelib/centerstring.py (2.7.12)
File  Edit  Format  Run  Options  Window  Help
str = "My name is unknown.";

print "str.center(40, 'b') : ", str.center(40, 'b')
```

When you click 'Run', and then 'Run Module', a new
shell will appear with these results:

```
Python 2.7.12 Shell
File  Edit  Shell  Debug  Options  Window  Help
Python 2.7.12 (v2.7.12:d33e0cf91556, Jun 27 2016, 15:19:22) [MSC v.1500 32 bit (
Intel)] on win32
Type "copyright", "credits" or "license()" for more information.
>>>
============== RESTART: C:/Python27/Lib/idlelib/centerstring.py ==============
str.center(40, 'b') :  bbbbbbbbbbMy name is unknown.bbbbbbbbbb
>>>
>>>
```

4. find ( ), or find (str, beg=0, end=len(str))

This is used to find a string in a string or substring.
The second code specifies that the search starts
from the beginning and end of the string.

str – specifies the string to find

beg – indicates the beginning of the search,
which is 0 (start)

end – indicates the length of the string. If this is not indicated, by default, it would be up to the end of the string.

Example:

str1 = "My name is unknown.";

str2 = "name";

print str1.find(str2)

print str1.find(str2, 7)

print str1.find(str2, 40)

See image below:

After you click 'Run', and then 'Run File', these results will be displayed in a new shell.

```
                                    Python 2.7.12 Shell              -  □  ✕
File  Edit  Shell  Debug  Options  Window  Help
Python 2.7.12 (v2.7.12:d33e0cf91556, Jun 27 2016, 15:19:22) [MSC v.1500 32 bit (
Intel)] on win32
Type "copyright", "credits" or "license()" for more information.
>>>
=============== RESTART: C:/Python27/Lib/idlelib/findstring.py ===============
3
-1
-1
>>>
>>> |
```

The results show -1, meaning the specified string
does not exist.

Again, keep in mind the simple string commands, such as:

print stringname[0] = prints the string's first character

print stringname = prints the whole string

print stringname *4 = prints the whole string 4 times.

print stringname + "Great Job! " = prints the whole string +
Great Job!

See image below:

```
Python 2.7.12 Shell                                      –  □  ☒
File  Edit  Shell  Debug  Options  Window  Help
Python 2.7.12 (v2.7.12:d33e0cf91556, Jun 27 2016, 15:19:22) [MSC v.1500 32 bit (
Intel)] on win32
Type "copyright", "credits" or "license()" for more information.
>>>
>>> mystring2="Tomorrow will be brighter!"
>>>
>>> print mystring2[0]
T
>>>
>>> print mystring2
Tomorrow will be brighter!
>>>
>>> print mystring*4

Traceback (most recent call last):
  File "<pyshell#7>", line 1, in <module>
    print mystring*4
NameError: name 'mystring' is not defined
>>> print mystring2*4
Tomorrow will be brighter!Tomorrow will be brighter!Tomorrow will be brighter!To
morrow will be brighter!
>>>
>>> print mystring2+"Great Job!"
Tomorrow will be brighter!Great Job!
>>>
>>> |
```

Observe from the image above that there was an error in the 3rd code (mystring*4) because the name of the string was wrong. That should have been mystring2.

When the error was corrected in the next print function, the result came out correct – the string was printed 4 times.

The other string commands are discussed in the other chapters.

These are some of the basic string operations that are useful for beginners. As you learn more about Python programming, you will learn about the more complex functions.

When you're ready to proceed to the more advanced methods, you can always access them from the Python program of your saved files.

Chapter 19: Symbols and Operators in Formatting Strings

You can format strings by using the symbols and operators. Chapter 21 has more examples of these operators.

For this particular chapter, the flag operators and integers will be discussed.

Types of integer presentation:

None   – indicates a decimal integer and outputs the number in base 10

'b'   - stands for **b**inary; it outputs the number in base 2.

'c'   - stands for **the c**haracter; it converts the integer (number) to a specified Unicode

                          character before printing.

'd'   - stands for **d**ecimal; it outputs the number in base 10.

'o'   - stands for **O**ctal format; it outputs the number in base 8.

'n'   - stands for **n**umber; its function is to insert the correct separator characters.

'x'   -stands for **Hex** format; for digits above 9, the lowercase letters are used. It

Outputs the number in base 16.

'X'   - this is the same as 'x', the difference only is that the uppercase letters are used,

for digits above 9.

Common flag characters used for strings:

You can also use conversion flag characters to format your strings. Here are the most common flag characters and their meaning:

'#' – this indicates that the value to be used is the alternate form as defined below.

'-' – this will override the 'o' conversion, if both are given. This indicates that the converted value is adjusted to the left.

'+' – this will override a 'space' flag. This is the opposite of the '-' flag.

'0' – this indicates that the values for the numeric values will be zero.

' ' – this blank flag is placed before an empty string or a positive number.

The old operator, %, allows easy formatting of strings. If this operator is still recognized by your Python version, here are some of its functions.

Here are some symbols that you can use with the operator %.

%s – conversion of string using str() before formatting.

%f – real number for floating point

%u- decimal integer (unsigned)

%g – the shorter of %e and %f

%G – the shorter of %E and %f

%e – lowercase 'e' (exponential notation)

%E – uppercase 'E' (exponential notation)

%c – character

%o – octal integer

%i and %d – decimal integers (signed)

%X – uppercase letters (hexadecimal integer)

%x – lowercase letters (hexadecimal integers)

Important Note:

In some new Python versions, curly brackets { } are used and the % is replaced by colons (:).

Example:

'%04.3f' will be changed with '{:04.5f}'

There are more complex string commands and codes, but for now, let's focus on these symbols and operators.

See more of the functions and operators through the examples in the other chapters.

Chapter 20: Important Python Semantics

Python has its own syntax and semantics. Before you can write or create your code, you have to be familiar with the Python language.

There are some differences in the Python version 2x and 3x. But generally, it uses some English words instead of punctuations. In this book, most of the discussions are focused on Python 2 because it's more commonly utilized. Python 3 has newer functionalities though, which will be discussed in some of the chapters.

Here are common Python statements and their uses:

1. **'off-side rule'** - where white space indentations, (increased - start or decreased - end), are utilized to indicate whether the block ends or starts.

2. **'pass'** - used as a code block.

3. **'if'** – executes a block of code. It can be used together with 'else'. A combination with 'else', gives the 'else-if' ('elif').

4. **'class'** – commonly used in project-oriented programming, and executing a block of code; the code can be attached to a class.

5. **'yield'** – this can be used as a statement and an operator. It is used to implement coroutines.

6. **'def'** – this statement defines a function or a method.

7. **'for'** – it iterates an object and indicates that the element/s can be utilized by the attached block.

8. **'assert'** – it's used to determine statements that should apply during debugging.

9. **'while'** – executes a block of code, as long as it's true.

10. **'with'** – it encloses a code block, and acquires a lock before the block of code is run.

11. **'try'** – this statement ascertains that the clean-up code black is run, and those exceptions are handled properly.

You can refer to chapter 6 for the type of Python statements.

Chapter 21: Operators and Their Functions

Operators are essential in writing your Python codes. Next we will go through the Logical and Comparison operators.

1. Logical operators

- **and** – (A and B) is FALSE. When you use the 'and' operator. Both conditions (A and B) should be true. If not, the result will display 'False'.

- **or** - (A and B) is TRUE. If one condition is true, the result will show
       "True'.

  Some programmers call them the Boolean Operators. They are used to connect sentences, present an option, or inclusion or exclusion of something.

2. Comparison operators (use to compare values)

!=	not equal
==	equal
>	greater than
<	less than
>=	greater than or equal to
<=	less than or equal to

You can use these operators with the 'if' statement, or in any syntax where they can be useful.

Reminder:

The symbol = means you're assigning a value, and == means you're comparing the values.

Example #1:

If 3<4:

print ('true')

If the statement is true, when you press 'enter' or execute, 'True' will be printed.

See image below:

You can also use the operators freely. Always press 'enter' to display results. See image below:

You can also use the 'and' operator this way to determine if the statements are 'true' or 'false'.

Example:

If 7>12 and 12>15:

If 7>12 or 12>15:

See image below:

Notice the different results for the 'and' and 'or' operators.

The 'in' operator can determine if the value is present in a string:

Example:

You have this in your string:

mystring=[1, 2, 3, 4, 5]

And you want to know if 1 is present in the string, simply enter this statement:

1 in string

And then press 'enter'. The result will display 'True', if 1 is indeed found in the string.

See image below:

```
>>>
>>>
>>> string = [1,2,3,4,5]
>>> 1 in string
True
>>>
```

The Python operators can help you create your modules or files. Use them freely and don't be afraid to experiment.

Python is still a developing language; you may be able to discover something new.

Chapter 22: Using 'IF ELSE' Statements

In Python, you can use various condition statements. However, you have to ascertain that you follow the Python syntax rules and indentation. One of these rules is to provide an indentation after the 'if' and 'else' statements, when you enter their codes. Simply press the tab once to provide the indentation.

Anyway, the program will assist you in determining errors in your Python syntax. If there's an error, it will display the errors, and what's wrong with them. You can also press for help, if you're lost in the sea of Python lingo.

Therefore, relax and enjoy the experience.

Functions

The 'IF ELSE' statements, which execute codes, are generally used to compare values, or determine their correctness. 'if' is expressed, if the condition is 'true', while 'else' is expressed when the condition is 'false'.

General code is:

if expression:

Statement/s

else:

Statement/s

Example:

Assign a base statement first. Let's say you're teaching chemistry to freshmen college students and you want to encourage them to attend your tutorials. You can compose this Python code:

```
hours = float(input('How many hours can you allot for your chemistry tutorials?'))
if hours < 1:
    print ('You need more time to study.')
else:
    print ('Great! Keep it up!')
```

print ('Chemistry needs more of your time.')

From your original Python shell open a New File where you can create your code. Write your code as shown in the image below:

Take not of the indentations and signs. Save the file, and click 'Run', and then "Run Module".

A new shell will appear, where you can test if your code is correct. In this example, this shell (box) will appear:

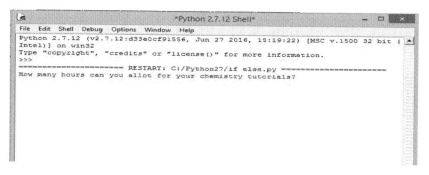

Your student or the user can then answer the question.

Let's say the student has decided to allot 3 hours for his tutorial, thus he typed 3.

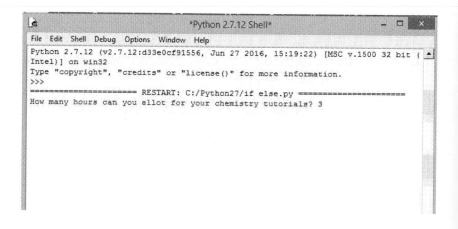

When the student presses 'enter' or execute, the result will print or display the 'if' and 'else' codes that you have specified.

Since the entered number is more than 1, the 'else' statement is printed or displayed.

See image below:

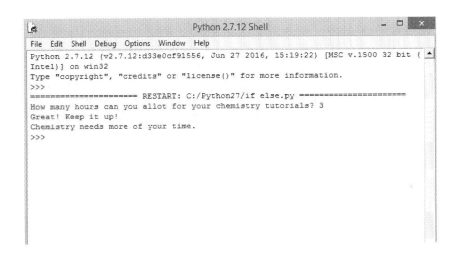

Reminders:

1. Always save any 'New File'.

2. Notice that the 'if' and 'else' statements are indented.

3. The 'if' statement is: print('You need more time to study.'), while the

   'else' statement is: print('Great! Keep it up!).

4. The 'if' statement will be printed, if the hours for tutorials inputted by

   the user is less than 1 hour; the 'else' statement will be printed if the hours for tutorials inputted is more than 1 hour.

5. Don't forget the colon (:), after the 'if'' and 'else' conditions.

6. You can have multiple codes/statements in your 'if' or 'else' conditions.

   Just remember to indent them.

7. Quotes are also used in the print functions, and parentheses have

enclosed the sentences to be printed.

In summary, the 'if' and 'else' statements are opposites. Either condition will be printed based on the condition given.

Chapter 23: Using ELIF Statements

The next type of statement is the 'elif' statement. "elif" is the combination of 'else' and 'if'.

These statements are used when there are more than two choices, and you want to compare various conditions.

The general Python syntax for 'elif' statements is this:

```
if condition1:
    Statement for condition1
elif condition2
    Statement for condition2
elif condition3
    Statement for condition3
elif condition4
    Statement for condition4
elif condition5
```

    Statement for condition5

else:

    Statement for false

Example:

You have encoded the grades of your students, and you want to give some encouraging words. You can compose the code below:

```
score=input('Type your grade in my subject.")

if score >= 75:
    print ('Passed. You can do better.')
elif score >= 80:
    print ('Good job.')
elif score >= 85:
    print ('Great!')
elif score >= 90:
    print ('Excellent.')
else:
```

print ('Failed. You still have the chance. Study harder')

See image below:

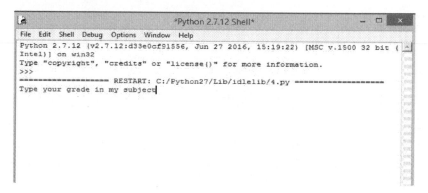

Save and click 'Run', and then 'Run Module'. A new shell will appear. See image below:

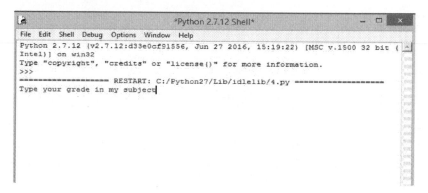

Your student can then enter his grade. If the grade of your student is 80, the result will print the statement you have specified in your code.

```
Python 2.7.12 Shell                                            – □ ✕
File  Edit  Shell  Debug  Options  Window  Help
Python 2.7.12 (v2.7.12:d33e0cf91556, Jun 27 2016, 15:19:22) [MSC v.1500 32 bit (▲
Intel)] on win32
Type "copyright", "credits" or "license()" for more information.
>>>
================== RESTART: C:/Python27/Lib/idlelib/4.py ==================
Type your grade in my subject.80
Passed. You can do better.
>>> |
```

You will notice that there's something wrong with the
code, because all the other values fall within the range
of the first 'if' statement.

You can remedy this by editing your syntax:

Grades = input('Type your grade in my
subject.')

if Grades >=75:

    print ('Passed. You can do better.')

if grades <75:

    print ('Failed. Keep studying.')

else:

    print ('Not enrolled.')

See image below:

```
grades2.py - C:/Python27/grades2.py (2.7.12)
File  Edit  Format  Run  Options  Window  Help
Grades = input('Type your grade in my subject.')

if Grades >=75:
    print ('Passed. You can do better.')
if grades <75:
    print ('Failed. Keep studying.')
else:
    print ('Not enrolled.')
```

If the student typed 75, the statement specified in your 'if' condition will appear.

See image below:

```
Python 2.7.12 Shell                                              –  □  ✕

File  Edit  Shell  Debug  Options  Window  Help
Python 2.7.12 (v2.7.12:d33e0cf91556, Jun 27 2016, 15:19:22) [MSC v.1500 32 bit ( ▲
Intel)] on win32
Type "copyright", "credits" or "license()" for more information.
>>>
===================== RESTART: C:/Python27/grades2.py =====================
Type your grade in my subject.
===================== RESTART: C:/Python27/grades2.py =====================
Type your grade in my subject.75
Passed. You can do better.
```

You can edit your Python code until you obtain the
desired results. It can be turn into a loop by adding
'while'. Refer to the chapter on loops.

Chapter 24: Functions of Python Loops

There are two types of Python loops; the 'while' and the 'for'. This word would be most probably new to you. But bear in mind that everything can be learned, and you will benefit tremendously with your basic knowledge of Python. So, cheer up and keep going.

What is a loop?

As defined in the previous chapter, it is a symbol used to represent repeated (iterated) word/s or sentence/s in Python programming. Anything that is being repeatedly used can employ a loop (a piece of code). Hence, it facilitates the task that you would want to accomplish.

Types of loops

1. **The 'while' loop** – this is used to implement a piece of code repeatedly.

Example:

Let's say you have these values: a – for individual numbers; t – for sum of the numbers:

```
a=1

t=0
```

And you want the user to 'Enter numbers to add to the total.', you write the code for the 'while; loop this way:

> print ('Enter numbers to add to the total.')

> print ('Enter x to quit.')

(Now use the 'while' function to allow the action to become repetitive.)

> while a ! = 0:

>> print ('Current Total: ', t)

>> a = float(input("Number? '))

>> a = float (a)

>> t+ = a

> print ('Grand Total = ', t)

You'r code will look like this.

Example:

> a=1

>> t=0

> print ('Enter numbers to add to the total.')

> print ('Enter x to quit.')

>> while a ! = 0:

>>> print ('Current Total: ', t)

$$a = \text{float}(\text{input}(\text{``Number? '}))$$

$$a = \text{float}\,(a)$$

$$t+ = a$$

$$\text{print ('Grand Total = ' , t)}$$

See image below:

```
1.py - C:/Python27/Lib/idlelib/1.py (2.7.12)

File  Edit  Format  Run  Options  Window  Help
a=1
t=0
print ('Enter numbers to add to the total.')
print ('Enter x to quit.')
while a!=0:
    print ('Current Total:   ' , t)
    a = float(input('Number? '))
    a = float(a)
    t += a
print ('Grand Total = ' , t)
```

Then, click 'Run', and then 'Run Module'. The box below will appear:

```
>>>
=================== RESTART: C:/Python27/Lib/idlelib/1.py ==========
=========
Enter numbers to add to the total.
Enter x to quit.
('Current Total:  ', 0)
Number?
=================== RESTART: C:/Python27/Lib/idlelib/1.py ==========
=========
Enter numbers to add to the total.
Enter x to quit.
('Current Total:  ', 0)
Number?
```

This code will allow the user to enter his number and the program will compute for the total.

The user can also subtract numbers, and the program will still get the total.

Let's say that the user has entered the following numbers: 1289, 6709 and 45678, the results will appear this way:

```
=================== RESTART: C:/Python27/Lib/idlelib/1.py ==========
=========
Enter numbers to add to the total.
Enter x to quit.
('Current Total:  ', 0)
Number? 1289
('Current Total:  ', 1289.0)
Number? 6709
('Current Total:  ', 7998.0)
Number? 45678
('Current Total:  ', 53676.0)
Number?
                                                    Ln: 82  Col: 8
```

The program or code continues, and a user can add (enter) as many numbers as he wants.

The loop will continue obtaining the sum of the entered numbers, repeatedly, until you press 'x' to 'exit'.

413

You or any user can also subtract numbers (examples – 90, and then -3456) and the loop will display the total.

See image below:

```
================== RESTART: C:/Python27/Lib/idlelib/1.py ==========
=========
Enter numbers to add to the total.
Enter x to quit.
('Current Total:   ', 0)
Number? 1289
('Current Total:   ', 1289.0)
Number? 6709
('Current Total:   ', 7998.0)
Number? 45678
('Current Total:   ', 53676.0)
Number? 879
('Current Total:   ', 54555.0)
Number? -90
('Current Total:   ', 54465.0)
Number? -3456
('Current Total:   ', 51009.0)
Number? |
```
Ln: 88 Col: 8

The code is useful, as long as 'x' is not entered. Once 'x' is entered, the loop will end and the program won't be useful anymore - unless you save it.

In these examples, you have to apply the basic rules in Python syntax, or statement.

Look out for the double parentheses. Use the function 'print', whenever you want your reader, or user to read the text, and don't forget to enclose your variables or elements in quotes.

2. The second type is the 'for' loop.

The 'for' loop can be used in printing elements, one by one. An example is this:

b= (9, 4, 2, 8, 12, 5, 67)

If, you want to print the numbers above, one by one, you can use the 'for' loop, this way:

for num in b:

(num – holds the values of each element in b.)

Hence, your final code would be:

for num in b:

print (num)

See image below:

For the 'while' loop, the condition must be true to be able to operate; unlike for the 'for' loop; it works even if the condition is not true.

Chapter 25: Creating and Using Tuples

Tuples as defined earlier, are similar to strings. Tuples and strings are the same - you cannot modify them because they are immutable (unchangeable).

This is because once you have assigned the values, they can no longer be changed. There are methods to the create new Tuples and strings though, as mentioned below.

Differences of Tuples and Lists

Lists use square brackets [ ], while Tuples use parentheses ( ). Heterogeneous data is also possible with Tuples. On the other hand, lists usually have homogenous data.

Uses of Tuples

1. When the data are converted to tuples, it can return values in groups. Generally, without Tuple, 'returns' provide only a single value.

2. They can be used as dictionary keys because they are immutable.

3. They are protected from accidental modifications.

4. Iteration is quicker with Tuples because of their nature.

5. They allow the grouping of related data that may be different in data types.

Built-in functions

There are built-in functions for Tuple that you must know. These are:

1. **tuple(seq)** – this is an important function because it can convert your lists to Tuples.

   Example: If you want to convert your list1 to tuple

   list1 = ('Vivian Dixon', 'single', 25)

   tuple(list1)

   See image below:

   ```
   >>>
   >>> tuple(list1)
   ('Vivian Dixon', 'single', 25)
   >>>
   >>>
   ```

   When you print it, the results will be:

   ```
   >>>
   >>> print tuple(list1)
   ('Vivian Dixon', 'single', 25)
   >>>
   >>>
   ```

2. **cmp(tuple1, tuple2)** – this function can compare two Tuples.

   Example:

   tuple1- ('cde',325)

   tuple2 – ('fgh', 525)

   cmp(tuple1, tuple2)

3. **min(tuple)** – it shows the minimum values found in your Tuples.

   Example:

   tuple=(3,6,9,11,13,15,20)

   min(tuple)

   print min(tuple)

   See image below:

```
>>>
>>> tuple=(3,6,9,11,13,15,20)
>>>min(tuple)
>>> print min(tuple)
3
>>>
>>> |
```

4. **max(tuple)** – it shows the maximum values found in your Tuples.

Example:

tuple =(1256, 1259, 1224, 1231, 1214)

max(tuple)

print max(tuple)

You can also press 'enter', after max(tuple), and the maximum value will appear, which is 1259.

See image below:

```
>>>
>>>
>>> tuple =(1256, 1259, 1224, 1231, 1214)
>>> max(tuple)
1259
>>>
>>> |
```

If you have decided to open a 'New File', you can access the results, by clicking 'Run' and then. 'Run Module'.

See image below:

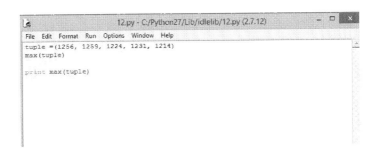

After you have clicked 'Run', and 'Run Module', the result will appear in a new shell:

See image below:

```
================= RESTART: C:/Python27/Lib/idlelib/12.py =================
1259
>>>
>>>
```

The same result will appear, which is 1259.

5. **len(tuple)** – it specifies the total lengths of your Tuples.

Example:

tuple =(1256, 1259, 1224, 1231, 1214)

len(tuple)

print len(tuple)

See image below:

```
12.py - C:/Python27/Lib/idlelib/12.py (2.7.12)
File  Edit  Format  Run  Options  Window  Help

tuple =(1256, 1259, 1224, 1231, 1214)
len(tuple)

print len(tuple)

|
```

When you click 'Run', and 'Run Module', the results will appear in a new shell, which is 5.

```
================== RESTART: C:/Python27/Lib/idlelib/12.py ==============
5
>>>
>>>
>>>
```

If you decide to use the original shell, without creating a 'New File', be sure to observe the correct indentation because your statement or code might not be able to work.

```
>>> tuple =(1256, 1259, 1224, 1231, 1214)
>>> len(tuple)
>>>
>>> print len(tuple)
5
>>>
>>> |
```

You will be obtaining the same results, whatever method you decide to use.

But for beginners, creating a 'New File' is advisable because you can edit your code all you want, before running it.

Changing Tuples

Tuples are immutable; however, Tuples can be sliced using a bracket [ ] and a colon (:), and concatenated or combined using the + sign. If the data type is mutable, the nested elements can also be changed.

The elements in a Tuple can be repeated, as many times as you want, with the operator (*) asterisk.

Creating Tuples

Step #1 – Place all elements inside the parentheses ( )

All the items that you would want to convert to a Tuple must be separated by commas, and enclosed by parentheses.

423

When the number-element is only one, the ending comma must still be added, to indicate that the data is a tuple.

Examples:

tup1 = ( )

tup2 = ("Jean", "Walker", 2004, "female", "fourth year");

tup3 = ("October", 20, 2014, "Saturday");

tup4 = (2, 3, 4, 5, 6, 7, 8, 9, 10);

Notice that the first Tuple is empty, and tup3 has integers, and word elements inside the parentheses.

The words are enclosed in quotes'; separated by commas, and all items are enclosed inside parentheses. It can also contain lists, floats and other items.

Some programmers don't use the parentheses to enclose the items in a Tuple. Choose what's more convenient for you.

When elements are not enclosed in parentheses (Tuples) or square brackets (strings), they are automatically identified as Tuples.

Step #2 – Access the values of your Tuples

You can assess the values of your Tuples by printing them. Based on the values of your Tuples above, you can choose what to print.

Keep in mind that your indexes in Tuples is the same as your lists – they start at 0.

Example:

print "tup2[2]: ", tup2[2]

print "tup3[1:3]: ", tup3[1:3]

See image below:

```
tup1 = ( )
tup2 = ('Jean', 'Walker', 2004, 'female', 'fourth year');
tup3 = ('October', 20, 2014, 'Saturday');
tup4 = (1, 2, 3, 4, 5, 6, 7, 8, 9, 10);

print "tup2[2]: ", tup2[2]
print "tup3[1:3]: ", tup3[1:3]
```

tup1.py - C:/Python27/Lib/idlelib/tup1.py (2.7.12)

File   Edit   Format   Run   Options   Window   Help

A 'New File' was created for these statements, so click 'Run' and then 'Run Module'.

The results will appear in a new shell.

See image below:

```
Python 2.7.12 Shell                                    -  □  ×

File  Edit  Shell  Debug  Options  Window  Help

Python 2.7.12 (v2.7.12:d33e0cf91556, Jun 27 2016, 15:19:22) [MSC v.1500 32 bit (
Intel)] on win32
Type "copyright", "credits" or "license()" for more information.
>>>
=================== RESTART: C:/Python27/Lib/idlelib/tup1.py ===================
tup2[2]:   2004
tup3[1:3]:  (20, 2014)
>>>
```

Keep in mind that the 1:3 indicates that the items printed will start at 1 up to 2, and not 3.

In the example above, the items are numbered this way:

tup2 = (#0 -"Jean", #1-"Walker", #2- 2004, #3 -"female", #4 -"fourth year");

Thus, #2 in tup2 = 2004 (which was printed)

tup3 = (#0 - "October", #1 - 20, #2 - 2014, #3 - "Saturday");

Thus, tup3[1:3] = 20, 2014 (which was printed)

This is because #1 is 20 and #2 is 2014; (1:3 is actually 1 to 2 only, and not 1 to 3). If you want to print 'Saturday', you have to change it to [1:4]

Deleting Tuples

As mentioned repeatedly, you cannot delete a Tuple file, but you can create a new one, and omit the elements you don't want to include. You can then delete the whole Tuple by using the key 'del'.

Example:

tup2 = ("Jean", "Walker", 2004, "female", "fourth year");

print tup2

See image below:

```
>>> tup2 = ('Jean', 'Walker', 2004, 'female', 'fourth year');
>>> print tup2
('Jean', 'Walker', 2004, 'female', 'fourth year')
>>>
```

Then add the statement for deletion:

del tup2;

print "after deleting tup2 : "

print tup2

When you enter, print tup2, the result below will appear:

```
>>>
>>> print tup2

Traceback (most recent call last):
  File "<pyshell#16>", line 1, in <module>
    print tup2
NameError: name 'tup2' is not defined
>>> |
```

Your tup2 file is no longer accessible because it has been deleted.

Updating Tuples

As previously mentioned, the elements in Tuples cannot be changed. Nonetheless, you can update your Tuples by getting items from your old Tuples to create a new Tuple.

Example:

tup5 = tup2 + tup3

print tup5

See image below:

```
>>>
>>> tup5=tup2 + tup3
>>> print tup5
('Jean', 'Walker', 2004, 'female', 'fourth year', 'October', 20, 2014, 'Saturday
')
>>>
>>>
```

When you press 'enter', the result is a new Tuple (tup5), composed of the elements of tup2 and tup3.

Now, let's proceed to the basic operations for Tuple. What are these operations that you need as you start to learn Python? Here they are:

Basic Operations

The basic operations for Tuple are the same with strings.

1. **Repetition** – use the key (*), asterisk.

Example:

tup2 = ("Jean", "Walker", 2004, "female", "fourth year");

tup2*2

When you press 'enter', the result would be:

```
>>>
>>>
>>> tup2 = ("Jean", "Walker", 2004, "female", "fourth year");
>>> tup2*2
('Jean', 'Walker', 2004, 'female', 'fourth year', 'Jean', 'Walker', 2004, 'femal
e', 'fourth year')
>>>
```

The elements of tup2 have been printed twice, as specified by your statement (tup2*2).

2. **Concatenation** – use the key (+) plus sign.

   Example:

   tup2 = ("Jean", "Walker", 2004, "female", "fourth year");

   tup3 = ("Clinical Chemistry", 80,);

   print tup2 + tup3

See image below:

A 'New File' was opened, therefore, the 'Run' and 'Run Module' menu was clicked. The result that came up in a new shell was the combination of the elements of tup2 and tup3.

```
Python 2.7.12 Shell                                              -  □  x
File  Edit  Shell  Debug  Options  Window  Help
Python 2.7.12 (v2.7.12:d33e0cf91556, Jun 27 2016, 15:19:22) [MSC v.1500 32 bit (
Intel)] on win32
Type "copyright", "credits" or "license()" for more information.
>>>
==================== RESTART: C:/Python27/Lib/idlelib/11.py ====================
('Jean', 'Walker', 2004, 'female', 'fourth year', 'Clinical Chemistry', 80)
>>>
>>>
```

3. **Iteration** – it works the same way as strings.

4. **Length** – it works the same way as strings, using the key, 'len'.

```
>>>
>>> len((1, 2, 3))
3
>>>
>>>
```

You can always refer to the strings chapter anytime you want to.

Chapter 26: How to Convert Python Data

In Python programming, data can be converted from one type to another. Here are simple steps of doing this.

For converting an integer to a character, use the key 'chr', like this:

Example:

chr(x)

Where 'chr' stands for character, and x stands for the integers (numbers).

Let's say you want to convert the integers: 13, 4, 10, 7 and 14. Simply type the key 'chr' and substitute the numbers for the x value.

Example:

chr(13)

chr(4)

chr(10)

chr(7)

chr(14)

When you press 'enter' the numbers are converted into characters. See image below:

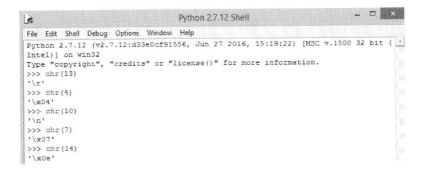

For converting to a string representation, use the key – 'str'.

Examples:

str(14)

str(23)

str(29)

The result will be:

```
>>>
>>>
>>> str(14)
'14'
>>> str(23)
'23'
>>> str(29)
'29'
>>>
```

For converting data to a tuple, use the key 'tuple'. If you want to convert data 'y' and 'x' to tuples, here are the codes:

Examples:

tuple(string1)

tuple(names1)

The statement above will convert the files string1 and names1 to Tuple files.

See image below:

```
>>>
>>> tuple('string1')
('s', 't', 'r', 'i', 'n', 'g', '1')
>>>
>>>
>>> tuple('names1')
('n', 'a', 'm', 'e', 's', '1')
>>>
>>> |
```

For converting data to a list, use the key, 'list'. For example, you want to convert the data, 'names1' to a list, this code/statement applies:

Example:

List('names1')

The file names1 is converted into a list file. See image below:

```
Python 2.7.12 Shell                                    —  □  ✕

File  Edit  Shell  Debug  Options  Window  Help
Python 2.7.12 (v2.7.12:d33e0cf91556, Jun 27 2016, 15:19:22) [MSC v.1500 32 bit (
Intel)] on win32
Type "copyright", "credits" or "license()" for more information.
>>>
>>> list('names1')
['n', 'a', 'm', 'e', 's', '1']
>>>
>>> |
```

For converting data to a frozen set, use the key, 'frozenset'. If your data is 'names1' and you want to convert it to a frozen set, see the example below.

Example:

frozenset('names1')

When you press 'enter', names1 will be converted to a frozenset. See image below:

```
>>>
>>>
>>> frozenset('names1')
frozenset(['a', 'e', 'm', 'n', '1', 's'])
>>>
>>>
```

For converting data to a set, use the key 'set'. An example is when you want to convert your data, 'names1', to a set, your statement would be:

Example:

set('names1')

The result would be:

For converting data to an expression string, use the key 'repr'.

Example:

If you want to convert your 'names1' file into an expression string, here's your code:

Example:

repr('names1')

After you press 'enter', the result will be this:

```
>>>
>>> repr('names1')
"'names1'"
>>>
>>> |
```

For converting your data (integer) to a Unicode character, you can use the key 'unichr'.

Example:

unichr(23)

When you press 'enter', the result will be:

```
>>>
>>> unichr(23)
u'\x17'
>>>
>>>
```

For converting one character to its integer value, you can use the key – 'ord'.

Example:

Convert your data ('a') to its integer value. Use this statement:

> ord('a')
>
> ord('b')
>
> ord('c')

When you press 'enter', these will be the results:

```
>>>
>>>
>>> ord('a')
97
>>>
>>> ord('b')
98
>>>
>>> ord('c')
99
>>>
```

For converting string data to an integer, use the key 'int'. If you want to convert a string, with a base, to an integer, use this code instead:

int(s[,base]).

Substitute your data for s.

Here are other conversions that may prove useful to you:

1. **eval(str)** – this returns an object, after evaluating your specified string.

2. **dict( )** -   this creates a dictionary, the value inside the parentheses must be in sequence.

3. **float ( )** – converts the integer or the value inside the parentheses to a floating-point number.

4. **oct( )** – converts the integer or number inside the parentheses to an octal string.

For more complex conversion keywords, you can learn them later on when you have become familiar with these common conversion keys. You can refer too to the other chapters in this book.

Chapter 27: How to Build Your Python Lists

In Python, lists can contain different types of data, such as string values, integers, and other various forms. They can also be iterated (repeated) several times. They can work as arrays, as well.

You can create any list you want and add or remove values from your list. Here's how:

Step #1 – Create your list

You can start creating your lists by using these codes:

```
mylist = [ ]
```

You're using blank brackets to indicate that there's still no value to your list. You can assign any value; in this example, we will be adding names to the list.

Example:

mylist = ['Wilson', 'White', 'Bronson']

When you have typed mylist, and have pressed 'enter', or execute, the contents of your 'mylist' will be displayed. See image below:

```
Python 2.7.12 Shell                                    – □ ×
File  Edit  Shell  Debug  Options  Window  Help
Python 2.7.12 (v2.7.12:d33e0cf91556, Jun 27 2016, 15:19:22) [MSC v.1500 32 bit (
Intel)] on win32
Type "copyright", "credits" or "license()" for more information.
>>> mylist = []
>>> mylist = ['Wilson', 'White', 'Bronson']
>>> mylist
['Wilson', 'White', 'Bronson']
>>>
```

Remember to enclose your variables with quotes and then brackets.

Take note that the index for the first item is 0, the next item is 1, the next item is 3, and so forth.

In the above example, the index for 'Wilson' is 0; 'White' is 1, and 'Bronson' is 3.

So, if you want to access 'Wilson', you can enter:

Examples:

mylist [0]

For 'White':

mylist [1]

and for 'Bronson':

mylist [2]

See image below:

```
┌─────────────────────────────────────────────────────────────────┐
│ ▌                    Python 2.7.12 Shell           ─  ⬜  ✕      │
├─────────────────────────────────────────────────────────────────┤
│ File  Edit  Shell  Debug  Options  Window  Help                  │
│ Python 2.7.12 (v2.7.12:d33e0cf91556, Jun 27 2016, 15:19:22) [MSC v.1500 32 bit ( ▲│
│ Intel)] on win32                                                 │
│ Type "copyright", "credits" or "license()" for more information. │
│ >>> mylist = []                                                  │
│ >>> mylist                                                       │
│ []                                                               │
│ >>> mylist=['Wilson', 'White', 'Bronson']                        │
│ >>> mylist                                                       │
│ ['Wilson', 'White', 'Bronson']                                   │
│ >>> mylist[0]                                                    │
│ 'Wilson'                                                         │
│ >>> mylist[1]                                                    │
│ 'White'                                                          │
│ >>> mylist[2]                                                    │
│ 'Bronson'                                                        │
│ >>> |                                                            │
│                                                                  │
└─────────────────────────────────────────────────────────────────┘
```

You can do it in reverse, by using the (-) sign.

Examples:

To access 'Wilson', type:

mylist [-3] and press enter.

To access 'White, type:

445

mylist [-2] and type enter.

To access 'Bronson', type:

mylist [-1]

Step #2 – Add to your list

You can also add to your list by using the 'append' function.

Example:

mylist.append ('Cruise')

When you press enter, the item will be added to your list.

Another example is when you want to add the name 'Park' to your list, use the same function:

Example:

mylist.append('Park')

In the image below, there was an error with the first execution because brackets were used.

It's important to note that when an error occurs in your code or syntax, the results will appear in red.

When the error was corrected by enclosing 'Park' with parentheses, the result was given correctly.

See image below:

```
>>> mylist.append('Cruise')
>>> mylist
['Wilson', 'White', 'Bronson', 'Cruise']
>>> mylist.append['Park']

Traceback (most recent call last):
  File "<pyshell#9>", line 1, in <module>
    mylist.append['Park']
TypeError: 'builtin_function_or_method' object has no attribute '__getitem__'
>>> mylist.append('Park')
>>> mylist
['Wilson', 'White', 'Bronson', 'Cruise', 'Park']
>>> |
```

Step #3 – Delete or remove an item from your list

You can do this by using the function keyword 'remove'.

Example: If you want to remove 'Bronson', you use the statement below.

mylist.remove ('Bronson')

You can continue removing from your list ('Wilson'), using the same function word.

mylist.remove('Wilson')

This statement will remove 'Bronson' and 'Wilson' from your list.

See image below:

```
>>>
>>>
>>> mylist.remove('Bronson')
>>> mylist
['Wilson', 'White', 'Cruise', 'Park']
>>>
>>> mylist.remove ('Wilson')
>>> mylist
['White', 'Cruise', 'Park']
>>> |
```

Remember to add a dot (.) between the name of your list and the function word.

There are other built-in function words (extend, max, len, print), you can use to edit or change your list. You can also print more than one list simultaneously.

Example:

print ('mylist1, mylist2, mylist3)

Chapter 28: Slicing from a List

You can 'slice' your list, to create a new list. Slicing is taking a portion, or selecting (slicing) a part of your list to display.

Keep in mind that the index of your list starts with 'o' (zero).

Example #1:

If you want to slice your list of names, you can use a colon (:) to do this. Let's say the name of your list is 'mylist2', and the values you assigned are: b, a, c, d, e, f, g, h, i.

Your syntax would appear this way:

mylist2 = ['b', 'a', 'c', 'd', 'e', 'f', 'g', 'h', 'i']

See image below:

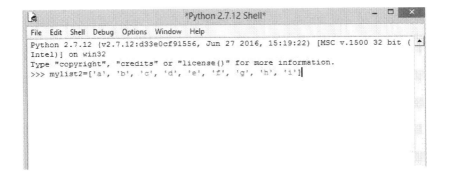

Call (Recall) the data by typing 'mylist2', and then press enter. Your list will appear.

See image below:

```
Python 2.7.12 Shell                                    —  □   ×
File  Edit  Shell  Debug  Options  Window  Help
Python 2.7.12 (v2.7.12:d33e0cf91556, Jun 27 2016, 15:19:22) [MSC v.1500 32 bit (
Intel)] on win32
Type "copyright", "credits" or "license()" for more information.
>>> mylist2=['a', 'b', 'c', 'd', 'e', 'f', 'g', 'h', 'i']
>>>
>>> mylist2
['a', 'b', 'c', 'd', 'e', 'f', 'g', 'h', 'i']
>>> |
```

You can slice this list by using the colon sign.

If you want to print from values 'b' to 'e', you can type:

mylist2 [1:5]

This is because, as previously explained, your indexes start from 0 onwards. Thus, 'a' is zero (0), 'b' = 1, 'c' = 2, and so forth.

When you press 'enter' or execute, the values, 'b' to 'e', will appear.

See image below:

```
                         Python 2.7.12 Shell               –  □  ×

File  Edit  Shell  Debug  Options  Window  Help
Python 2.7.12 (v2.7.12:d33e0cf91556, Jun 27 2016, 15:19:22) [MSC v.1500 32 bit (
Intel)] on win32
Type "copyright", "credits" or "license()" for more information.
>>> mylist2=['a', 'b', 'c', 'd', 'e', 'f', 'g', 'h', 'i']
>>> mylist2
['a', 'b', 'c', 'd', 'e', 'f', 'g', 'h', 'i']
>>> mylist2 [1:5]
['b', 'c', 'd', 'e']
>>>
```

There is always an option to edit your entry, if you got
the wrong files.

Let's say you want the 'f' values to be included in your
print list, just make use of the code:

mylist2[1:6]

And press enter.

See image below:

```
                                Python 2.7.12 Shell          –  □   ×
File  Edit  Shell  Debug  Options  Window  Help
Python 2.7.12 (v2.7.12:d33e0cf91556, Jun 27 2016, 15:19:22) [MSC v.1500 32 bit (▲
Intel)] on win32
Type "copyright", "credits" or "license()" for more information.
>>> mylist2=['a', 'b', 'c', 'd', 'e', 'f', 'g', 'h', 'i']
>>>
>>> mylist2
['a', 'b', 'c', 'd', 'e', 'f', 'g', 'h', 'i']
>>> mylist2 [1:6]
['b', 'c', 'd', 'e', 'f']
>>> |
```

You can also use this statement, as a shortcut:

mylist2[1:]

Leaving the second value blank after the colon, will
mean you want to access the values up to the last item
in your particular list.

See the last portion of the image below:

```
Python 2.7.12 Shell                                          - □ ×
File  Edit  Shell  Debug  Options  Window  Help
Python 2.7.12 (v2.7.12:d33e0cf91556, Jun 27 2016, 15:19:22) [MSC v.1500 32 bit (
Intel)] on win32
Type "copyright", "credits" or "license()" for more information.
>>> mylist2=['a', 'b', 'c', 'd', 'e', 'f', 'g', 'h', 'i']
>>>
>>> mylist2
['a', 'b', 'c', 'd', 'e', 'f', 'g', 'h', 'i']
>>> mylist2 [1:6]
['b', 'c', 'd', 'e', 'f']
>>>
>>> mylist2[1: ]
['b', 'c', 'd', 'e', 'f', 'g', 'h', 'i']
>>> |
```

You can leave the space before the colon blank to indicate that you want to access/print from 0 of the values.

Example:

mylist2[:7]

When you press 'enter' or execute, this will appear: See the last entry (bottom portion of the shell.

```
Python 2.7.12 Shell                                              –  □  ×
File  Edit  Shell  Debug  Options  Window  Help
Python 2.7.12 (v2.7.12:d33e0cf91556, Jun 27 2016, 15:19:22) [MSC v.1500 32 bit (
Intel)] on win32
Type "copyright", "credits" or "license()" for more information.
>>> mylist2=['a', 'b', 'c', 'd', 'e', 'f', 'g', 'h', 'i']
>>>
>>> mylist2
['a', 'b', 'c', 'd', 'e', 'f', 'g', 'h', 'i']
>>> mylist2 [1:6]
['b', 'c', 'd', 'e', 'f']
>>>
>>> mylist2[1: ]
['b', 'c', 'd', 'e', 'f', 'g', 'h', 'i']
>>>
>>> mylist2[ :7]
['a', 'b', 'c', 'd', 'e', 'f', 'g']
>>> |
```

You can print the whole list too, if you want, by leaving
blanks, before and after the colon.

Example:

mylist2 [:]

Press 'enter', and all the values in your list will be
displayed. See image below:

```
                              Python 2.7.12 Shell              -  □   x
File  Edit  Shell  Debug  Options  Window  Help
Python 2.7.12 (v2.7.12:d33e0cf91556, Jun 27 2016, 15:19:22) [MSC v.1500 32 bit (
Intel)] on win32
Type "copyright", "credits" or "license()" for more information.
>>>
>>> mylist2 = ['a', 'b', 'c', 'd', 'e', 'f', 'h', 'i']
>>> mylist2
['a', 'b', 'c', 'd', 'e', 'f', 'h', 'i']
>>>
>>> mylist2[ : ]
['a', 'b', 'c', 'd', 'e', 'f', 'h', 'i']
>>> |
```

You can also use the negative sequence of indexing, using the (-) sign. Please refer to the previous chapter.

Example:

If you want to slice your list to only 'h', you can enter in your shell this statement:

mylist2 [-2:7]

You can also enter:

mylist2 [-2:]

to print 'h' and 'i'.

See image below:

```
Python 2.7.12 Shell                                    – ☐ ✕
File  Edit  Shell  Debug  Options  Window  Help
Python 2.7.12 (v2.7.12:d33e0cf91556, Jun 27 2016, 15:19:22) [MSC v.1500 32 bit (
Intel)] on win32
Type "copyright", "credits" or "license()" for more information.
>>>
>>> mylist2 = ['a', 'b', 'c', 'd', 'e', 'f', 'h', 'i']
>>> mylist2
['a', 'b', 'c', 'd', 'e', 'f', 'h', 'i']
>>>
>>> mylist2[ : ]
['a', 'b', 'c', 'd', 'e', 'f', 'h', 'i']
>>>
>>> mylist2[-2:7]
['h']
>>> mylist2[-2: ]
['h', 'i']
>>>
```

Skipping values in your list:

If you want to skip some values, you can use an additional colon to identify the values you want to skip.

Let's say you want to skip the values after every two intervals, you can use this code:

Example:

mylist2 [0:8:2]

Press 'enter', and the value, after every one interval, will be omitted from your results.

See image below:

```
>>>
>>>
>>> mylist2[0:8:2]
['a', 'c', 'e', 'h']
>>>
>>>
```

You can also make use of this code, if you want the same results (after every one interval).

mylist2 [: :2]

When you press 'enter', you will be getting the same results. See image below:

```
>>>
>>>
>>>
>>> mylist2[ : :2]
['a', 'c', 'e', 'h']
>>>
>>> |
```

You can use every 1, or 2 intervals, or any interval you want. Simply edit the code to obtain or print your desired results.

Example #2

If you have these assigned values to your list:

mylist =[2, 3, 4, 5, 6, 7, 8, 9, 10, 11, 12, 13, 14, 15]

Press 'enter', and then type mylist to display your values. See image below:

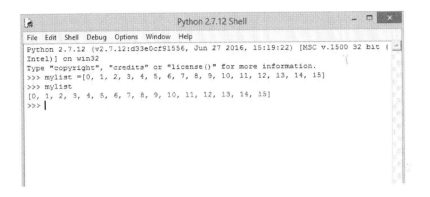

Take note that these numbers represent the indexes of your files. Hence, they may contain different data types, such as strings and other variables.

So, let's say you want to print/display files (indexes) 2 to 11 from your list, you can use a colon (:) to do this.

Example:

mylist [2:12]

Press 'enter' or execute. The values from 2 to 11 will be displayed.

See image below:

```
Python 2.7.12 Shell                                    –  □  ×
File  Edit  Shell  Debug  Options  Window  Help
Python 2.7.12 (v2.7.12:d33e0cf91556, Jun 27 2016, 15:19:22) [MSC v.1500 32 bit (
Intel)] on win32
Type "copyright", "credits" or "license()" for more information.
>>> mylist = [0, 1, 2, 3, 4, 5, 6, 7, 8, 9, 10, 11, 12, 13, 14, 15]
>>> mylist
[0, 1, 2, 3, 4, 5, 6, 7, 8, 9, 10, 11, 12, 13, 14, 15]
>>> mylist [2:12]
[2, 3, 4, 5, 6, 7, 8, 9, 10, 11]
>>>
```

In the example above, the list displayed is only up to 11, but you entered 12 in your statement. Hence, if you want your result to display up to 12, your statement should be:

mylist [2:13]

Press 'enter', or execute. The results will display your files from 2 to 12. Index 13 will not be displayed.

See image below:

```
Python 2.7.12 Shell
File  Edit  Shell  Debug  Options  Window  Help
Python 2.7.12 (v2.7.12:d33e0cf91556, Jun 27 2016, 15:19:22) [MSC v.1500 32 bit (
Intel)] on win32
Type "copyright", "credits" or "license()" for more information.
>>> mylist = [0, 1, 2, 3, 4, 5, 6, 7, 8, 9, 10, 11, 12, 13, 14, 15]
>>> mylist
[0, 1, 2, 3, 4, 5, 6, 7, 8, 9, 10, 11, 12, 13, 14, 15]
>>> mylist [2:12]
[2, 3, 4, 5, 6, 7, 8, 9, 10, 11]
>>>
>>> mylist[2:13]
[2, 3, 4, 5, 6, 7, 8, 9, 10, 11, 12]
>>> |
```

These are the basic ways to slice your list. You will be able to learn more as you continue advancing in your knowledge of Python.

Explore

Now, try creating your own modules. Creating a python module can be easy or difficult depending on your ability to follow the advice given to you.

Modules in python must have a .py extension to make it functional. Here is how you can use to create your module:

1. **Set up the framework of your module**.

   You could take an already developed module and enhance it.

   Example:

   ```
   cd modules/unsupported
   cp example bird
   ```

2. **Revise the files**

   You need to alter the files to fit the objective of your module.

3. **Configure your pom.xml**

   Replace the word "example" with the title of your module :

   ```
   <name>Example</name>
   ```

4. **Add your code to the directory**

5. **Let others know that you are about to launch your module**

   This is important since this is a way of getting support from others who are into programming who can help you improve your module.

6. **Run it/Test your module**

   Let your module run for the purpose you developed it. This is also to test whether your module is working or not

Did it work?

Hopefully, it did!

Chapter 29: Short Quiz on Python Programming

To test whether you have learned something from this book, here's a short quiz. Don't pressure yourself. Take a deep breath and relax. Learning should be fun. Take your time answering these questions without reviewing your notes.

You can write your answers on a piece of paper, or if you have already downloaded your free Python Programming application, you can answer the questions, using your interactive shell.

Questions:

1. You are tasked to prepare a Python program/module in welcoming college freshmen to your Business Administration Department. How can you let the students input their names, their ID numbers, and the time they came in, in the Python shell? How can you let them access your welcome message?"

2. What key can you use to convert an integer (number) to a string?

3. What is the simplest data/file form that is best in creating a list of names?

4. Create a Python statement that can print the following:

a. A Tuple file named "taxRecord' that has these values: taxRecord=('first payment', 2015, 'second payment', 2016)

   names= ("John", "Bill", "Donna", "Ted", "Lance") + ages=(20, 30, 18, 25, 30)

b. items "c", "d", "e", "f" & "g" from this list: mylist=("a", "b", "c", "d", "e", "f", "g", "h", "I", "j")

c. the length of this list: grocery = ('egg', 'sugar', 'milk', 'butter', 'flour')

5. How do you obtain the answer of 89^{12}, using a Python function key?

6. What is the Python function or key that you will use, if you want to remove a value from a list? Give one example.

7. Define concatenation. Give one example.

8. Create a Python statement based on the following:

a. Print the contents of var1 30 times; var1=("Today is the day.")

b. Access the built-in modules.

c. Change the string file, 'records' to a Tuple file;

   records = ['Grace', 'Lancaster', 30, 'Metro St Chicago']

9. What is the difference between = and == ?

10. True or False: Python programming is an object-oriented language.

That's it!

Chapter 30: Answers to Short Quiz

Let's see if you got the correct answers. There may be slight differences for the various Python versions; nevertheless, it won't hurt you to learn about the answers.

ANSWERS:

1. This is the first lessons in the book – allowing a user to input some data.

    You can either click the Python shell directly from your saved Python file:

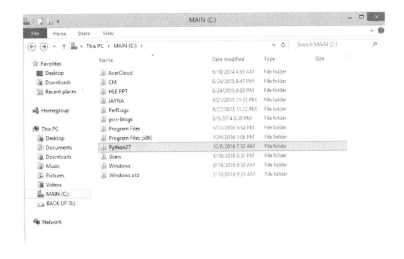

Then, click on python.

See image below:

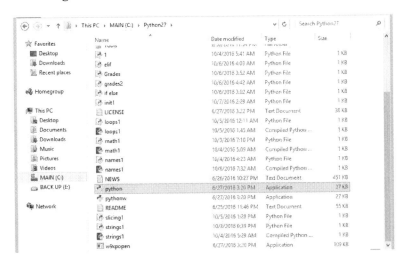

To open your shell:

You can also do it the long way, but have a clearer and more maneuverable shell. Refer to chapter 7.

Let's say you have opened already your Python shell below using the long method:

Open a 'New File' as instructed in chapter 7. Hence, you click 'File', and then 'New File' on the upper left-hand corner of your shell. The new shell will appear:

In this new shell, you can edit all you want because pressing the 'enter' key won't return anything yet, unless you press or click the 'Run' menu. In this shell, you can now enter your Python statements.

The question is asking how you can allow the freshmen students to input their names, their ID numbers and the time they came in, and receive or access your welcome message.

The main fact to remember is that you use the 'input' key whenever you are asking the user to input or type something.

In your 'New File' shell, create these statements:

a=str(input("Please type your name and enclosed it in double quotes, an press enter."))

b=int(input("Please enter your ID number, and press enter."))

c=int(input("Please enter the time you came in, and press enter."))

print (max(a,b,c))

print ("Thank you. Welcome to the College of Business Administration, where learning is fun!")

Then you run this Python statement/code by clicking 'Run', and then 'Run Module'.

The first question will appear in a new shell. See image below:

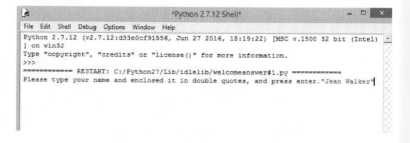

Let's say the name of the student is Jean Walker, so she enters it. When she presses enter, the new question will appear:

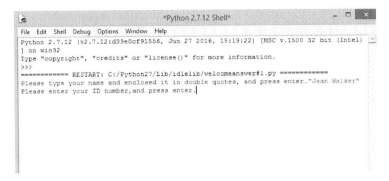

Let's say Jean's ID number is 3401. After she types in her ID, the next question will appear.

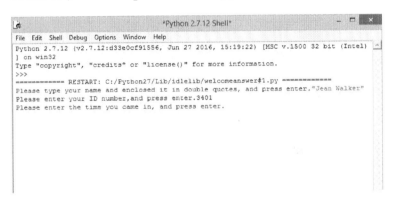

If the time that she came in was 7, so she types it.

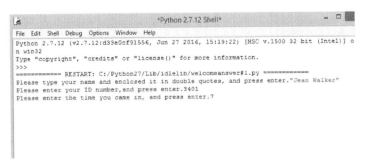

After the student presses enter, this will appear:

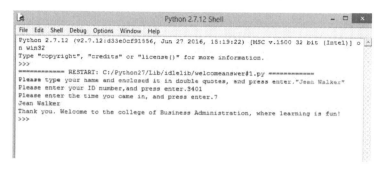

```
Python 2.7.12 Shell
File  Edit  Shell  Debug  Options  Window  Help
Python 2.7.12 (v2.7.12:d33e0cf91556, Jun 27 2016, 15:19:22) [MSC v.1500 32 bit (Intel)] o
n win32
Type "copyright", "credits" or "license()" for more information.
>>>
=========== RESTART: C:/Python27/Lib/idlelib/welcomeanswer#1.py ===========
Please type your name and enclosed it in double quotes, and press enter."Jean Walker"
Please enter your ID number,and press enter.3401
Please enter the time you came in, and press enter.7
Jean Walker
Thank you. Welcome to the college of Business Administration, where learning is fun!
>>>
```

Of course, you will have to be there to assist. You have to save the file of each student after he is done, and 'Run Module' for the next student.

This would be tedious, but after this beginner's lesson, you may want to learn advanced lessons later on, on how to embed the program and let it run by itself.

2. The key is str(int). For example you want to convert 10 to a string, you just use this statement: str(10).

3. The simplest best data/file form that is best in creating a list of names is a 'list'. This is because you can modify or update the information, if you want.

4. a. The Python statement in printing a Tuple file named "tacRecord" would be:

taxRecord=('first payment', 2015, 'second payment', 2016)

print "taxRecord"

```
>>>
>>>
>>> taxRecord=('first payment', 2015, 'second payment', 2016)
>>> print taxRecord
('first payment', 2015, 'second payment', 2016)
>>> |
```

b. The Python statement/code would be:

names= ("John", "Bill", "Donna", "Ted", "Lance")

ages=(20, 30, 18, 25, 30)

print (names + ages)

This will print/return your desired results:

```
Python 2.7.12 Shell                                          -  □  ×
File  Edit  Shell  Debug  Options  Window  Help
Python 2.7.12 (v2.7.12:d33e0cf91556, Jun 27 2016, 15:19:22) [MSC v.1500 32 bit ( ▲
Intel)] on win32
Type "copyright", "credits" or "license()" for more information.
>>> names=("John", "Bill", "Donna", "Ted", "Lance")
>>> ages=(20, 30, 18, 25, 30)
>>> print (names+ages)
('John', 'Bill', 'Donna', 'Ted', 'Lance', 20, 30, 18, 25, 30)
>>>
>>> |
```

c. The Python statement/code would be:

mylist=("a", "b", "c", "d", "e", "f", "g", "h", "i", "j")

print mylist[2:7]

When you press 'enter', the items, "c", "d", "e", "f", & "g" will be printed from the list:

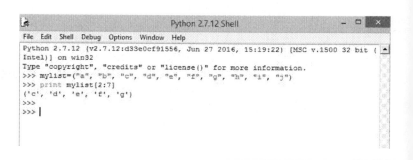

d. The Python statement/command/code would be:

grocery = ("egg", "sugar", "milk", "butter", "flour")

print grocery

When you press 'enter', the results will be the printing of the items in your grocery list.

('egg', 'sugar', 'milk', 'butter', 'flour')

```
Python 2.7.12 Shell
File  Edit  Shell  Debug  Options  Window  Help
Python 2.7.12 (v2.7.12:d33e0cf91556, Jun 27 2016, 15:19:22) [MSC v.1500 32 bit (
Intel)] on win32
Type "copyright", "credits" or "license()" for more information.
>>> grocery = ("egg", "sugar", "milk", "butter", "flour")
>>> print grocery
('egg', 'sugar', 'milk', 'butter', 'flour')
>>>
>>>
```

If you receive an error after pressing 'enter', your Python version may want you to use double quotes, so just edit your entries.

5. To obtain the answer of 89^{12} or 89 raised to the 12th power is to use the key 'pow'.

Hence:

pow=(89,12) or 89**12

press 'enter' or 'Run', 'Run Module' (if 'New File').

```
Python 2.7.12 Shell
File  Edit  Shell  Debug  Options  Window  Help
Python 2.7.12 (v2.7.12:d33e0cf91556, Jun 27 2016, 15:19:22) [MSC v.1500 32 bit (
Intel)] on win32
Type "copyright", "credits" or "license()" for more information.
>>> pow(89,12)
246990403565262140303521L
>>>
>>>
```

6. The Python function or key to remove a value is 'remove'. Let's say your list is this: phone, diary, pen, notebook, pencil; and you want to remove dairy from your list, here's how.

Example:

myList1=['phone', 'diary', 'pen', 'notebook', 'pencil']

```
Python 2.7.12 Shell                                        – □ ×
File  Edit  Shell  Debug  Options  Window  Help
Python 2.7.12 (v2.7.12:d33e0cf91556, Jun 27 2016, 15:19:22) [MSC v.1500 32 bit (
Intel)] on win32
Type "copyright", "credits" or "license()" for more information.
>>> myList1=['phone', 'diary', 'pen', 'notebook', 'pencil']
>>>
```

Now, remove 'diary' with this statement:

myList1.remove("diary")

```
Python 2.7.12 Shell                                        – □ ×
File  Edit  Shell  Debug  Options  Window  Help
Python 2.7.12 (v2.7.12:d33e0cf91556, Jun 27 2016, 15:19:22) [MSC v.1500 32 bit (
Intel)] on win32
Type "copyright", "credits" or "license()" for more information.
>>> myList1=['phone', 'diary', 'pen', 'notebook', 'pencil']
>>> myList1.remove('diary')
>>>
```

When you print it, the results will no longer show the value 'diary'. You can do this by entering the statement:

print myList1

And then press 'enter'. The results will print myLsit1 without 'diary'. See image below:

```
Python 2.7.12 Shell                                    - □ ×
File  Edit  Shell  Debug  Options  Window  Help
Python 2.7.12 (v2.7.12:d33e0cf91556, Jun 27 2016, 15:19:22) [MSC v.1500 32 bit (
Intel)] on win32
Type "copyright", "credits" or "license()" for more information.
>>> myList1=['phone', 'diary', 'pen', 'notebook', 'pencil']
>>> myList1.remove('diary')
>>> print myList1
['phone', 'pen', 'notebook', 'pencil']
>>>
>>>
```

7. In the Python language (as defined in chapter 3), concatenation is a series of connected strings or variables use in Python programs. The small strings can become larger strings through concatenation. This can be done using the 'join'( ) procedure, or the (+) sign. To replicate the string, you can use the asterisk (*) symbol, together with the number of how many times it should be replicated. (mystring1*10).

Example:

If you want the data: a, b, c and 4, 5, 6 to connect to each other, or to join each other. You can use the statement below:

['a', 'b', 'c'] + [4, 5, 6]

When you press 'enter', the two strings are already joined. See image below:

```
[Python 2.7.12 Shell]
File  Edit  Shell  Debug  Options  Window  Help
Python 2.7.12 (v2.7.12:d33e0cf91556, Jun 27 2016, 15:19:22) [MSC v.1500 32 bit (
Intel)] on win32
Type "copyright", "credits" or "license()" for more information.
>>> ['a', 'b', 'c'] + [4, 5, 6]
['a', 'b', 'c', 4, 5, 6]
>>>
>>> |
```

8. a. You can print the content of var1 30 times with the asterisk (*) function. The statement would be:

var1=('Today is the day.')

print var1*30

```
>>>
>>> var1=('Today is the day.')
>>> var1*30
>>> print var1*30
Today is the day.Today is the day.Today is the day.Today is the day.Today is the
 day.Today is the day.Today is the day.Today is the day.Today is the day.Today i
s the day.Today is the day.Today is the day.Today is the day.Today is the day.To
day is the day.Today is the day.Today is the day.Today is the day.Today is the d
ay.Today is the day.Today is the day.Today is the day.Today is the day.Today is
the day.Today is the day.Today is the day.Today is the day.Today is the day.Toda
y is the day.Today is the day.
>>>
>>> |
```

Hence, whether the value is an integer or a literal string, the (*) function works.

If an error appears like this one: "SyntaxError: EOL (End of the Line) while scanning string literal", it means your strings are too long. You can do any of the following:

- Check your quotes, change it to single or double quotes as the case may be.

- Check your distances between your values, they may be too far apart.

480

- Check your quotes, some may have missing quotes or unmatched quotes.

- Add the slash sign "\", if your values are too long, or the triple quotes if your statements are too long.

b. To access the built-in modules, the Python statement would be:

help('modules')

When you press enter, Python will ask you to wait as the program gathers all the built-in modules. You won't wait a minute because after several seconds, the results will return all the built-in modules. See image below:

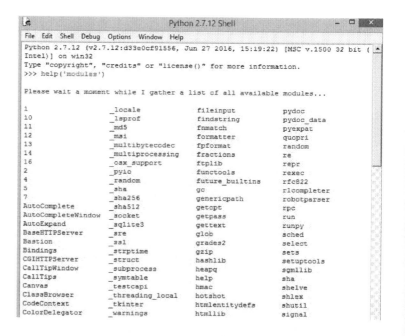

c. You can change a string file to a Tuple file by simply using the function, tuple(str). The statement would be:

```
records = ['Grace','Lancaster',30,'Metro St Chicago']

tuple(records)

print tuple(records)
```

See image below:

This is a 'New File', so click 'Run", and then 'Run Module', and a new shell will open with the results. Your string file, 'records' is converted to a Tuple file.

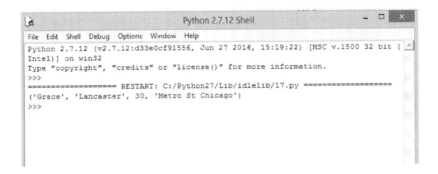

9. The difference between = and == is that the = (equal sign) is used to give/assign values to data or files, while the == (double equal sign) is used to indicate that the values are equal.

10. True. Everything in Python refers to an object. That's its advantage over another programming language.

Now check your answers, and score yourself:

Here's how to score yourself:

1. 10 points

2. 3 points

3. 3 points

4. a. 5 points

   b. 5 points

   c. 5 points

5. 5 points

6. 5 points

7. 5 points

8. a. 3 points

   b. 3 points

   c. 4 points

9. 2 points

10. 2 points

Total points = 60

Score Interpretation:

60 points = Excellent! You're a genuine Python - follower.

You can now proceed to advance lessons.

45-59 points = Congratulations! You can be proud of your knowledge.

30-44 points = You've passed the test! You can do better though.

Keep going!

<30 points = Heads up! Failure is not permanent. It just means going

for it again, and again, until you succeed!

Chapter 31: Pointers in Using Python Programming

To optimize your use of the Python program as a beginner, here are significant pointers that can help your learning activity become fruitful.

1. **Be positive.** Anything new can be daunting – especially a 'foreign' language. Think about learning Korean, Chinese or Spanish, and you won't even want to start. But optimism can make you change your mind. As Master Yoda from "Star Wars' said: *"Do, there is no try."* Believe that you can do it, and you can. Think about all the benefits you can derive from what you will learn.

2. **Python is an extensive program; continue learning.** What we have discussed here is only the tip of the iceberg. There are still thousands of complex information about Python that you can learn.

3. **If you want to obtain several values from a list, use the 'slice' function**, instead of using the index. This is because the 'index' can provide you a single value only.

4. **Assign only integer values to indices.** Other number forms are not recognized by Python. Keep in mind that index values start from zero (0).

5. **Remember to use the 'help' function whenever necessary**. Explore the 'help' function, when in doubt on what to do. A little help from Python can go a long way.

6. **Python programming is a dynamic language.** Thus, you can experiment and come up with a code of your own to contribute towards its advancement.

7. **There are some differences among the Python versions**. But don't fret, the program itself has built-in modules and functions that can assist you in solving the problems you can encounter.

8. **The interactive shell can promptly return results**. That's why it's preferable to open a 'New File' first, before creating your statement. But if you're sure of your code, then, go ahead, and use the interactive shell directly.

9. **Separate your multiple statements, in a single line, with semicolons**. This is easier and more sensible.

10. **The three 'greater than' signs (>>>) or arrows is a prompt from the interactive shell.** You can explore their functionality as you create your statements.

11. **The Python interpreter can act as a calculator.** Using your interactive shell, you can compute math problems quickly – and continuously. No sweat!

12. **The # symbol indicates that the statement is a comment**. The # sign is placed before the comment, and after the Python statement, so Python won't mistake it as part of the statement or code.

13. **Use the reverse or backslash (\ ) to escape a single quote, or double quotes.** Examples of these are contracted words, such as 'don't, "won't", 'aren't'. When using them in Python, they will appear this way: 'don\'t', "won\'t", 'aren\'t'.

14. **A short cut in joining two literal strings (strings literal) is to put them beside each other and enclose each in quotes.** Example: 'Clinical' 'Chemistry'. This will give: ClinicalChemistry.

```
>>>
>>> 'Clinical' 'Chemistry'
'ClinicalChemistry'
>>>
>>>
>>> |
```

15. **For modifying immutable data, create a new file.** These immutable data include strings, numbers, frozen set, bytes and Tuples. By creating a new file, you can modify, add and remove items from your immutable data.

Conclusion

The information in this book has the purpose of teaching you simple statements/codes that you can use easily.

It's expected that by this time, you can create the basic statements or codes for Python. In addition, you must be able to save and run your files on your own.

Remember to explore and test your short snippets of codes by using Python's interactive shell.

If you happen to be an expert, then the basic contents of this book may serve as reminders of the Python language.

For you, dear beginner, it's not a crime to go back to the chapters that you still could not comprehend.

By all means, you can read it twice, or as many times as you want.

After all, you can only truly learn about a new language, when you keep practicing.

Therefore, improve your knowledge by doing these three things regularly with Python: practice, practice and practice!